Wakarusa
Community School
Library

YO-AGR-407

J. EDGAR HOOVER, MODERN KNIGHT ERRANT

Other Books in the Men of Achievement Series:

Herbert Hoover, Humanitarian

Ernest Hemingway, Man of Courage

Conrad N. Hilton, Hotelier

J. Edgar Hoover, Modern Knight-Errant

Dr. Albert Schweitzer, Medical Missionary

Carl Sandburg, Poet and Patriot

Lowell Thomas, Adventurer

Charles F. Kettering, Inventor and Idealist

Bob Mathias, Champion of Champions

Frank H. Krusen, M.D., Pioneer in Physical Medicine
and Rehabilitation

J. C. Penney, Merchant Prince

Nathaniel Leverone, Pioneer in Automatic
Merchandising

Harry A. Bullis, Champion American

John Foster Dulles, Peacemaker

William L. McKnight, Industrialist

Lyndon B. Johnson, Man of Reason

Norman Vincent Peale, Christian Crusader

General Carlos P. Romulo, Defender of Freedom

Edgar James Helms, the Goodwill Man

J. EDGAR HOOVER,
Modern Knight Errant

A Biographical Sketch of the Director of the F.B.I.

by

MILDRED HOUGHTON COMFORT

Publishers

T. S. DENISON & COMPANY

Minneapolis

171-B+T-921 400 10-73

Copyright ©, 1959, by

T. S. DENISON & COMPANY, INC.

All rights reserved, including the right to reproduce this book, or portions thereof, except that permission is hereby granted to reviewers to quote brief passages in a review to be printed in magazines and newspapers, or for radio and television reviews.

First Printing—January 1958
Second Printing—June 1959
Third Printing—May 1960
Fourth Printing—June 1961
Fifth Printing—March 1962
Sixth Printing—November 1962
Seventh Printing—July 1963
First Revised Edition—March 1964
Ninth Printing—February 1965
Tenth Printing—July 1965
Eleventh Printing—January 1966
Twelfth Printing—July 1966
Thirteenth Printing—January 1967
Fourteenth Printing—October 1967
Fifteenth Printing—February 1968
Sixteenth Printing—November 1968
Seventeenth Printing—July 1969

Printed in the U.S.A.
BY THE BRINGS PRESS

International Copyright Secured
Library of Congress Catalog Card Number: 58-14402

The Library of Congress catalog entry for this book appears on page 130.

Wakarusa
Community School
Library

E. S. E. A.
TITLE II

CONTENTS

DEDICATION

To young Americans who are proud of their heritage and who are growing up in the fine traditions of courage, humor, and common sense.

Chapter I

A New Year's Welcome

Happy New Year! The greeting swelled out from the Capital of the United States over all the land. It was January first in the year 1895. The bells in the churches of Washington, District of Columbia, were proclaiming, not only a brand new year but, unknowingly, the birth of a child who was to become a modern Knight Errant in the cause of safety with liberty and justice for all. He was to wear on the shield of his personality the very words inscribed on the shield of the Federal Bureau of Investigation: "Fidelity, Bravery, Integrity."

He was to ride forth, not in shining armor—though, if he had worn armor, it would have been the most brightly polished of all—but in handsomely tailored clothes. Nor was he to go astride a horse, leaping over a moat, but in swift cars, fast trains, and speedy planes. And the moats he crossed were state lines. His nickname **Speed** was earned, not as a runner but as a worker whose chivalry demanded that he rid his country of kidnapers, extortionists and hijackers, and most of all, of un-Americans. For he was and is a patriot.

The place in which he was born was no castle or palace, but a very comfortable house of gray stucco. It was a family home, of two-and-a-half stories, with a high, wide veranda across the front and tall, lace-curtained windows looking out on Seward Square. It was around this Square that neighbors often saw older brother Dick wheeling his infant brother in a high baby buggy. Admirers who peeked in at the new baby would have seen a very dark-eyed infant in beautifully ruffled clothes that must have taken hours of ironing.

The address of the family house placed it in Precinct 5, South-East Washington, and, being in the District of Columbia where the national government was housed, it was not a voting precinct. Not being able to vote held one advantage. There was no prejudice, especially concerning political parties.

The child in the high baby buggy was the youngest of four and was christened John Edgar. The world today knows him as J. Edgar Hoover and people sometimes ask, "What does the J. stand for?" When assured that it stands for the substantial name of John, they are invariably satisfied.

J. Edgar Hoover was fortunate to have been born into a typical American family with old-fashioned learnings. Even as a very young child he was taught that **"Honesty is the best policy."**

His mother, Annie M. Scheitlin Hoover, was to be the most important influence in his life. She was a short, plump woman, a homebody whose warmth and understanding spread far beyond her own fireplace.

Many a man hired as a Special Agent by her son, basked in her tender smile and many of them affectionately called her Mother. Her motherliness, however, was not all mildness and gentleness. She was a strict parent, rearing her children in the tenets of the Lutheran Church and teaching them the Bible. They learned by heart the moral sayings in which she believed. It was taken for granted that they go to Sunday School and church. J. Edgar received a little Testament as a reward for attending Sunday School fifty-two consecutive Sundays, never once being late.

"It was one of my treasures," he says. "I still have it."

He can still remember an uncle reading a Bible lesson to him in that boyhood home, and he likewise remembers learning that his great-grandfather, on his mother's side, was John Hitz, first Swiss consul-general to the United States. And he was proud of a great uncle who worked as a stone mason on the United States Capitol.

Mrs. Hoover carried her home teachings beyond religious instruction into the wide, wide world of general knowledge. She had studied and traveled in Europe, but she was humble and without pretense. She laughed and she sang and she had the merry heart that "doeth good like a medicine."

J. Edgar's father was Dickerson N. Hoover, a hard-working, kindly man, chief of the printing division of the Coast and Geodetic Survey. John Edgar often walked to his father's office at closing time so that he could walk home with him. This affection between father and son was a precious thing and memorable, for the father died in 1921.

In the meantime, the other children had moved away, and John Edgar for seventeen years was his mother's sole support.

The family had never had a great deal of money, but as the boy remembered, they always had enough. From the time he was twelve, John Edgar worked at various jobs.

Let him tell the story of those first jobs himself. He said, "I started earning money when I was twelve years old by carrying groceries. In those days markets did not hire delivery boys, but I discovered that if one stood outside a store, a customer laden with purchases would happily accept a helping hand and gratefully tip anyone who aided with a heavy load. The first such commission I got was to carry two baskets two miles for which I received a tip of ten cents. I realized that the quicker I could complete each chore, the more money I could earn, so I spent most of my time running."

His running actually netted J. Edgar amazing profits for each day.

"Because I ran back to the market and was outside the Eastern Market every day after school and from seven A. M. to seven P. M. each Saturday, I could earn as much as $2 in a day. In those times that was a King's ransom."

He gave the money to his mother, but the value of this experience was not solely monetary. He learned to evaluate people, the generous and the greedy, the kindly and the stingy, the good-natured and the bad-natured. These lessons in observation prepared him to meet unusual situations and to handle many kinds of people all through the years ahead.

He attended grade school during the week and sang in the choir in his mother's church on Sundays. He taught Sunday School and so enjoyed the contacts with the children that he wanted to become a minister. A drain on the family's funds, caused by his sister's illness at the time John Edgar was ready to enter college, changed his plans for the ministry. He decided to get a daytime job and enter a night law school.

One thing he did have that would fit well either into the ministry or the law: he had a loud, clear, forceful voice. One school incident is told of a newcomer to the halls of learning asking, "What is that noise—a lion roaring?" and the reply, "Oh, that's only Hoover."

His voice was not only vigorous, but he spoke rapidly always. One reporter said, "I can take down two hundred words a minute, but J. Edgar Hoover speaks four hundred words a minute." That might be an exaggeration, but it is no exaggeration to say that he always spoke briskly and clearly and said what he had to say fast. Of himself he once said when criticized, "By nature I express myself vigorously at all times. I'm not a soft, easy-going individual. I play tennis hard. I walk fast. And in my testimony I spoke with vigor."

At this time he was talking before a committee in Congress. But the young boy had already shown the results of the careful molding of character that he always said **begins at home.** His mother, his father, his pastor and his teachers were training him for what lay ahead and he was an eager and serious learner.

Much later he was to say, "I find my own rules of conduct laid down in the 6th chapter, the 8th verse, of Micah. This says, 'And what doth the Lord require of thee, but to do justly and to love mercy, and to walk humbly with thy God.'"

Chapter II

Mr. Hoover's Schooling

J. Edgar Hoover's education began, as does the education of every child, in his home. Both Hoover parents were ambitious for their children, wanting them to gain knowledge and wisdom. J. Edgar pressed forward constantly in the world of learning, first in the public grade school and then in high school and college.

During these boyhood days, he developed a certain amount of hero worship. People were always to be a vital part in his life. Some people cared mostly about things; other people cared about ideas. But J. Edgar Hoover cared about people. He could never have been a hermit or a recluse, not this knight errant seeking new ways to serve his fellow man. He was too vital, too alive.

Two people stood out in his boyhood as his ideals: Dr. Donald Campbell McLeod, his pastor and Biff Jones, his coach. Dr. McLeod was a Christian of the first water with definite ideas. He taught the young men in his classes that they could be good Christians without being sissies. There was nothing of the sissy about J. Edgar Hoover to begin with, and he played ball with the same gusto that he did everything else.

It was during this time that a baseball smashed his nose. It was a serious accident and it gave his good, strong face the rugged appearance it has today. For some people such an accident would be a catastrophe. For J. Edgar Hoover it proved to be a distinction. No one would ever mistake him for anybody else.

He was and is an impressive person, with his husky build and his swift stride. His thick black hair is clipped and his black eyes glow with health, vitality, and power. Dr. McLeod had taught his boys that clean living and firm faith will work wonders in well-being. J. Edgar Hoover is proof of this teaching.

At the time he left the elementary grades, J. Edgar was of slight build. Biff Jones, the old Central High coach, had only to glance at the slender boy to realize that this eager newcomer was not football material. However, this boy had so much character that Biff Jones took a personal interest in him.

He advised him to go in for debating to exercise his mind and into the high school corps to train his body.

Immediately the debating team picked up steam, and the new boy orator gave stimulus to a lagging, disinterested group. The boys were talented enough, but now they began to do some thorough thinking about such problems of the day as the "fallacies of women suffrage." J. Edgar led them to twelve straight victories that were positively triumphs.

But his greater delight was in the high school corps into which Biff Jones had directed him. He became the Captain of Company A and proudly declared it to be "a rattling good military aggregation." He went about with these boys and had dates the same as the others, except that he never "went steady." They all teased him and accused him of being in love with Company A.

He graduated from old Central High in 1913 and immediately secured a job as a clerk in the Library of Congress. His beginning salary was $360 a year, his departing salary $840. One of the Library officials said, "I never saw such an eager, hard-working boy. I'm sure he would be Chief Librarian if he stayed with us."

The Library job was, of course, a daytime job. Nights he attended the George Washington University Law School.

He was "No. 1" in his fraternity, Kappa Alpha. The same sternness that had enabled him to improve the debating team and Company A in high school now came to the fore. As one member of Kappa Alpha expressed it, "J. Edgar Hoover took a **dim view** of such antics as crap games, poker, and drinking bouts." Instead of making him unpopular, his sane and sensible views won for him a grudging admiration. One of the most critical of the gay blades said, "It takes his sort of courage to build a finer America and we should find the courage to follow after and help him."

J. Edgar Hoover earned two degrees at George Washington University, his Bachelor of Laws degree in 1916—with honors—and his Master of Laws degree in 1917. During these years he developed a valuable friendship with Frank Baughman that was to last a lifetime. Frank was as easy-going as J. Edgar was dynamic. Frank was to become J. Edgar's aid from 1919 to 1948 when he retired. An incident Frank recalls with pleasure happened at the time he was shipped off to Army Camp in World War I. J. Edgar, accompanied by "Mother Hoover," came to the station to see him off. It was typical of the Hoovers that their friendships were never superficial but deep and lasting.

But J. Edgar Hoover's education for the great task which lay ahead, had not yet been completed. He was to have definite training for it. He joined the United States Department of Justice. As a clerk there he worked quietly but earnestly. The job assigned him was to prepare legal cases for the Assistant Attorney General, Francis P. Garvan.

The result of his accurate work on these papers produced some deportations of such aliens as Emma Goldman and over two hundred other undesirables. Bitter as she was over being sent back to Russia as an undesirable alien, Emma Goldman said, "At least J. Edgar Hoover was fair to me."

J. Edgar Hoover had not only done the "paper work." He went down the bay to see the **Buford** sail from New York on December 21, 1919. He was determined to see his task completed.

As the **Buford,** called the "Soviet Ark," pulled out,

a reporter made note of the concerned official from the Department of Justice and designated him as "that slender bundle of high-charged electric wire." That description has often been repeated.

By 1921 J. Edgar Hoover had become Assistant Director of the Bureau of Investigation as it was known in those days. Then Attorney General Harlan F. Stone, later to be Chief Justice of the United States, decided to move J. Edgar Hoover up, to make him Director of the Bureau of Investigation to replace the famous detective, William J. Burns.

J. Edgar had always admired Harlan F. Stone. The man was a brilliant jurist. And he was strictly honorable, one of the truly great, honorable men of his age. President Coolidge had appointed him to clean up the miserable state of affairs left by the Harding politicians.

That now-famous interview between J. Edgar Hoover and Harlan F. Stone happened in 1924. It is advisable to get the account of what actually happened from J. Edgar Hoover himself.

He said, "Mr. Stone was scowling when I came in. He was a rugged, gruff, but fair man. The scowl was a mannerism and not something in his personality. . . . I told him I would take the job as Director only on two conditions.

"He said, 'What are they?'

'I said the Bureau had to be divorced from politics, with appointments made solely on merit. Second, promotions would be made on proved ability. The F.B.I.

would not be a catch-all for political hacks and would be responsible only to the Attorney General.

"Mr. Stone scowled again and said, 'I wouldn't give it to you under any other conditions. That's all. Good day.'"

The "young man" that Harlan F. Stone appointed was only twenty-nine years old when he became Director of the Federal Bureau of Investigation.

J. Edgar Hoover had hit at the high goal toward which he had unconsciously moved. He would be forever grateful to the great Harlan F. Stone.

When Herbert Brownell became Attorney General, one of his first acts was to remove the huge oil portraits from his office walls. The walls, he said, were buckling from too many attorney generals.

J. Edgar Hoover asked for the one of Harlan F. Stone, to be hung in his own offices.

"Sure, Edgar," said Mr. Brownell, "But why that one?" Of course he knew why.

Chapter III

New Director Makes Great Changes

In the yearbook published by his high school class, J. Edgar Hoover was acclaimed "a gentleman of dauntless courage and stainless honor." Now, at twenty-nine, he was able to prove it.

The vigorous stride into the office of Director of the FBI marked the beginning of a great task.

J. Edgar Hoover still lived with his mother at 413 Seward Square, S. E., Washington, D. C., but he spent so much time in the Department of Justice that his office was like a second home. But one phase of his life was never to change. He believed with all his heart in the eternal moral rules his mother had taught him.

Almost his first act was to do away with the "buzzard's roost." The Buzzard's Roost was a room in the Justice Building where loafers gathered. For one thing, they swapped dirty stories, and it is said, that much as J. Edgar Hoover enjoyed humor, he never told an off-color story. He was disgusted with the filthy talk of men who were supposed to be an example in moral values in their country. Moreover, the loafers were forever helping to "polish off a bottle" that every Special Agent was supposed to furnish on his return from a case. The Director was disgusted, not only by the crude stories and the drinking, but also by the waste of time.

The Director had always been deeply religious, and he wanted his men to hold to a belief in God and to a righteousness in living.

The old-fashioned expression, "he worked like a beaver," was certainly true as J. Edgar Hoover got underway with his new job.

His next task was even less savory. He had to weed out the Special Agents who were unfit to belong to the FBI. Some of these men were ex-convicts themselves, but had wielded enough influence to get in. Some were plain riff-raff without education or any native ability. Many were hangers-on that politicians had rewarded with a job in return for favors. Of course there were a few dedicated men, and these men were of the caliber that J. Edgar Hoover wanted all along the line.

The new Director's popularity waned. He was even threatened and blamed for being a tyrant. But a merit system was substituted for the old hit-and-miss methods. If a man wanted to qualify, he had his chance. If he wanted to advance, he had only to earn that advancement.

At the time Mr. Hoover took over the Bureau, there were 657 employees, but when the Bureau was founded in 1908 there were less than 100 regular employees. Nor was the work broad even in its scope. The early workers spent their time ferreting out violations of anti-trust laws and bankruptcies, constantly examining ledgers. Frequently they showed an interest in white slaves and automobile thefts. But they worked without any authority.

Even the Special Agents who left their ledgers to work outside, were not equipped in any way. They could not carry weapons. They were not allowed to make arrests. If they did catch a criminal, they had to find a policeman or a United States marshal to arrest him. They had no automobiles. To get around they walked, ran, or used street cars. Naturally the public respect for them was never great; they were considered a joke.

J. Edgar Hoover changed every single condition that made an FBI man a subject for joking. Within a short time he was being respected by every American citizen and feared by every criminal in the country. Here were men who could not be bought, nor would they "listen to reason."

Every single Special Agent that came into the Bureau under J. Edgar Hoover came on merit alone. Not even a glowing letter of recommendation from a Congressman counted; the man himself had to qualify. Politicians soon ceased to pawn off their misfits on the FBI. J. Edgar Hoover was often criticized and condemned. It is said that under a Republican administration, he was accused of being a Democrat. Under a Democratic administration, he was accused of being a Republican. But never, during his three Republican and two Democratic administrations, was he ever accused of being a Communist. Even his worst enemies knew that he was an honest, loyal American.

He was to make many changes and improvements in the Bureau but none so important as the qualifications he demanded in his Special Agents. He chose them carefully, and he promoted them as they earned their promotions.

How can a man who wants to join the F.B.I. get into the Bureau? First of all, he must have reached his 23rd but not his 41st birthday on the date the application is filed. Secondly, he must be in good, even rugged health, and be able to pass a stiff physical examination. The third requirement is that he must be a citizen of the United States of America and be willing to work in any part of this country.

Even with these qualifications, he may not get to be one of J. Edgar Hoover's Special Agents. The requirements have tightened until now there are only two doors through which a man may enter.

The first entrance is because of a good law school education, and one must be a graduate, for a knowledge of law is invaluable in presenting cases. The F.B.I. does not try criminals but it gives information which is used as evidence.

The second door is through training in Statistics and Certified Public Accounting. Experts are needed to handle business records and to look into certain cases where bookkeeping is important. Bank thefts would come under this classification.

Not long ago a curious policeman asked a Special Agent this question: "Did you ever meet J. Edgar Hoover in person?"

The Special Agent replied, "Every Special Agent meets J. Edgar Hoover in person. And every man in the organization admires and respects his Chief. As a matter of fact, that is what they call him, the Chief."

Since Special Agents must meet all types of people, under various conditions, it is an advantage to have special talents or to know more than one language.

One case was solved by an agent who understood Italian and who overheard a telephone conversation in a spaghetti restaurant. Another case was solved by a man who went as a fiddler into hillbilly country. A third man, who had done much KP in the Army, hired out as a dishwasher. He became acquainted with a fellow-worker who was suspected of sending an extortion note to his boss. An Agent who could speak Swedish helped to solve a case of smuggled motorcars being shipped overseas. The list is endless.

Not only did J. Edgar Hoover choose his men carefully, but he gave them their work tools. He did not outfit them with false beards and mustaches or with green goggles, but with guns and the right to use them. Today every single Special Agent is issued a .38 caliber revolver by the F.B.I.

He has other modern weapons at hand, too. Also available for him are Thompson submachine guns, shotguns, rifles, pistols, tear-gun outfits, and bullet-proof vests and shields. His life is protected with all types of up-to-date equipment.

Each office has its own automobile. Trains and planes may be used without question. There are fifty-five field offices, spreading out all over the United States from Washington, D. C., to Los Angeles, California, and J. Edgar Hoover is in touch with all of them every day of the year.

The Bureau has become valuable and valued. J. Edgar Hoover is always ready to go into action with his Special Agents.

Chapter IV

The F.B.I. Academy

A new man has been approved by J. Edgar Hoover as a Special Agent in his FBI. He has good character, rugged health, and a thorough education. But that is not enough. The new man must be trained. Catching criminals requires a very special kind of training, not taught in any regular school in the United States.

The Director of the FBI has built up his own school. It is called F.B.I. Academy. It is located on the big reservation of the United States Marine Corps at Quantico. It lies among the wooded hills of Virginia.

The new Special Agent reports promptly, on the minute, as he must always report. He has already met the dynamic man, J. Edgar Hoover, looked into the shining black eyes of the straight, rugged Chief, and has felt himself standing a little taller, a little prouder. He has even seen the Chief's car of bullet-proof steel with windshield and windows an inch thick, and he realizes that the Chief is always in grave danger. He, too, will have to face danger on every trip to which he is assigned. His will not be an easy job.

A supervisor drives him out to Quantico. It is located about an hour's drive from Washington.

A sentry allows the car to pass along a broad roadway lined with buildings. Another half mile, and the new man sees the plain but useful buildings of the F.B.I. Academy.

He is allowed to go through the buildings, and the first thing he notices is the cleanliness and order. From floor to ceiling in every classroom everything shines. In the sleeping quarters pillows and blankets are placed in precise order. The dining room, where he lunches with the students, is pleasant, and the meal is served on linen with silver and glass and china as befits gentlemen.

During the fourteen-week course the Director insists that every man be taught the subjects that will insure success in his work and safety for himself. The new man is impressed with the program although at first he catches only a few familiar words like Defense Tactics, Bank Robbery, Extortion, Kidnaping, Communist, Espionage and Sabotage. Skillful use of firearms is emphasized. In the Academy Laboratories he will observe methods of detecting various kinds of fibers, soils, blood, and secret inks, and much more.

He visits a class where the men, in shorts and shirts, are going through vigorous setting-up exercises. They are warming up for a lesson on how to disarm an armed bandit.

This first lesson that he saw acted out he would never forget.

One of the young men was chosen to walk up to the instructor with a 38-caliber revolver and point it a few inches from his midriff.

The young man chosen did a good imitation of an ugly robber. He snarled in a voice full of venom, "Stick 'em up!"

Even as he spoke, he doubled up like a jack-knife, dropped his gun with a clatter, and hit the floor on his back with a resounding whack. He got up dazed, rubbing his gun hand with his free hand. There was a sort of foolish grin on his face though he winced.

"What happened?" he asked.

The instructor said, "I paralyzed your gun hand by pressing my thumb and finger into the tendons of your hand—hard."

"I'll say **hard**," the student agreed. "Then you knocked me over—hard again."

"You have to know how it feels," the instructor explained, "so you can be certain of the results you can expect when you have to deal with a criminal whose gun is poking your ribs. A G-Man never fires his gun except when his life or the life of somebody else is in danger. Then he shoots, and he shoots straight."

G-Man. The newcomer was aware that Special Agents were called G-Men, but he wondered where the name had come from.

The student who had played robber knew. As he

stepped back to give another man a tryout, he said,
"Machine-gun Kelly gave us that name. He was a
machine-gunner in the First World War—that's how
he got his name. He could have been a great guy, but
he became a cold-blooded killer. I've heard that he
spent sixty dollars a week just for the ammunition he
used in target practice. He thought of himself as a
great expert, but he was a coward. His specialty was
the tommy-gun and his hatred was Special Agents,
trained by J. Edgar Hoover."

"Go on," the new man urged, but the Special Agent
who was still rubbing his gun hand pressed his lips
tightly together.

Then he said, "It was not until 1934 that Congress
gave the FBI sufficient power to handle major crimes
—interstate, of course, crimes that were not to be
handled by local people. . . . And it wasn't long, I can
tell you, before the underworld began to feel the pressure. . . . When Charles Urschel, the millionaire Oklahoma oil man, was kidnapped, things began to happen
so fast that the criminals simply withered. . . . Can't
you just see Machine-gun Kelly shivering in a corner
as the F.B.I. Agents closed in on him?

" 'Don't shoot, G-Man!' he squealed.

" 'Don't shoot—what?' the Special Agent asked.

" 'G-Man—Government Man,' Machine Gun Kelly
explained, all the fight gone out of him."

It was very strange, the new Special Agent thought,
that one of the worst criminals on record should have

given the Special Agents a name that was to become famous. It was something fine to be a G-Man. If a G-Man started after somebody, he was bound to be caught. Everybody knew that.

The new Special Agent was taught, first of all, to be a good shot. He practiced both at indoor and outdoor targets. He learned to shoot at still targets and at moving ones. After awhile he could shoot standing, sitting, running, or jumping. His hardest task was to shoot from an automobile going over a rough road at high speed.

He studied from books. He learned from lectures by experts. J. Edgar Hoover employed only experts to teach. He learned from models, sand tables on which were buildings, trees, roads and even animals all in miniature. Looking at the sand table he had to figure out how he could close in on the criminals hiding in the farmhouse. Then he was sent out to a real farmhouse in the same setting and was given a chance to prove his cleverness. He had to know how to jump from an automobile, get behind a tree for protection, and shoot at the same time.

He had to know how to shoot at night as well as in the daytime, and how to judge distances. He may have had a favorite gun, but he had to be able to use different kinds and always to keep them in first-class condition.

Such an extensive course as this the young man took in his first fourteen weeks as a G-Man! He studied boxing and jujitsu. He learned photography. He became aware of the science used in detective work. He saw instruments that could detect what kind of a gun a bullet had been fired from. He was amazed that certain lights could show up hidden writing. He studied tire patterns and how to make a cast of a footprint. There were ways of studying ashes, dust, soil, cloth, bloodstains and hairs to determine what they were and where they came from. The dust or soil on a man's shoes, for instance, could reveal where he had been. Even dirt under fingernails could be analyzed. There might be a bit of blue thread, a trace of skin, or certain paint to reveal a fact. The newcomer could scarcely believe it when he saw a moulage, a reconstructed head that looked exactly like a murdered man.

The first training school was not the end of the newcomer's education, even though he was now a Special Agent, a G-Man. J. Edgar Hoover, as Chief, had instructed every man to come back for periodic retraining courses of two weeks' duration as there are always new discoveries and new ideas to pass on.

Chapter V

Fingerprints Used to Catch Criminals

Look closely at your fingertips, palm upward. Notice the tiny ridges with countless pores in them and running in odd curves. If you looked carefully, you would see similar ones on the palms of your hands and the soles of your feet. What did Nature intend them for? To help you seize and hold things. If your fingers were slippery smooth, it would be difficult even to pick up a pencil.

The unique thing about these ridges and patterns is that no two are alike. Nobody in all the world has fingerprints like yours. Look at them closely under a magnifying glass. The ball of the thumb and the tips of the fingers are best studied. Experts have names for the loops, arches, and whorls and divide the various types into eight classes in order to more easily record each person's fingers on card indexes.

J. Edgar Hoover did not discover fingerprinting but he has made better use of this knowledge than anybody in the whole world. Fingerprinting, he says, is

33

Wakarusa
Community School
Library

the only reliable means of identification of a person. When a thief is arrested, for example, his fingerprints are taken and compared with the fingerprints on the stolen article.

Once the Bertillon measurements were declared the best means of making certain the identity of an individual. This method was invented by Alphonse M. Bertillon, the noted French anthropologist and criminologist. He perfected his system of measurements in 1882, made photographs of his subjects, and wrote out careful descriptions as well. His method was followed by others.

But J. Edgar Hoover can show you the photographs of two prisoners who have exactly the same head measurements. Moreover, they look so similar that no one could tell them apart. But they do not have the same fingerprints. Twins and triplets and even quadruplets may have, to the casual onlooker, identical features and coloring, but they will not have the same fingerprints.

Fingerprinting is not new. Hundreds of years ago the people of China used this method of identification. They attached fingerprints to important papers and valuable packages. The method usually was to press a thumb print into soft wax and then attach it to paper or ribbon. The wise Chinese knew that nobody but the person concerned could make the same fingerprint.

Nor does one know how old the hand drawing on the cliff in Nova Scotia might be. It must have been made, historians say, by an Indian, long before the white man came to the land. This hand shows clearly the ridges of a fingerprint.

A man by the name of Dr. Henry Faulds is supposed to have discovered the fact that every individual has a different fingerprint. Scotland Yard in England was interested and began a study of the subject. Sir William Herschel and Sir Francis Galton gave it their close attention. But it was Sir E. R. Henry who used the new knowledge in a practical way. It is not surprising that he became Commissioner of Police of Scotland Yard.

In our own country our police officers soon gave up Bertillon methods and accepted fingerprinting as an easy and sure way of identification.

It was in the year 1924, when J. Edgar Hoover took over as Director of the FBI, that the files—now called the master records—were opened to the national police force and could be used by every police department all over the country. The files were enlarged. The National Bureau of Criminal Identification added their records to the ones already set up by the F.B.I. Then Leavenworth Penitentiary added theirs. Now on file in J. Edgar Hoover's offices are nearly 44,000,000 fingerprints of persons arrested. This represents 15,160,987 different individuals. As of December 1, 1963, there were on file in the F.B.I. 169,052,831 sets of fingerprints of which 43,922,599 were arrest-type fingerprints.

There are other files just as valuable. The F.B.I. has 324,779 nicknames on file. Blackie, Shortie, Red, Doc, and Winkie are quite common. Others are ironically descriptive, such as "Honest Mary," "Chair

Pusher," and "Dingaling."

This nickname group is classified alphabetically. Some are kidnapers, some are extortionists, and some are murderers.

Another interesting file has to do with personal appearances and habits. These files include information of physical deformities, scars, moles, dentures— everything from the color of the eyes to mannerisms and a way of walking. Clothes are described, brands of cigarettes smoked, and choices of liquor. Places of entertainment may run from a dive, a hangout, or a cellar to an elegant home or opera house. One may expect the jewel thief to appear at a club or the opera, and he may even wear evening clothes with a flower in his buttonhole.

Whether he knows it or not, the thief will be traced. The stolen property file includes valuable furs, silver, and jewels. It is only a matter of a short time when the thief will be caught along with the fences who handled the stolen goods and the dishonest people who bought them. For the goods stolen must be turned into cash in order to be used. A man with marked bills in his pocket may walk the streets hungry, not daring to use the bills. A man with a stolen car may not dare to park for fear of being caught. A woman with lovely jewels dare not wear them.

Again and again J. Edgar Hoover emphasizes the fact that criminals seldom, if ever, have anything to show for their misdeeds. Even bank robbers who have stolen huge sums of money are not free to use the loot. They must divide with fellow criminals, pay for hide-outs and protection. Many a crook is glad when it is all over. Of course he must pay the penalty for his wrong-doing, but he does not have to live in constant fear, not only of the law but of his own henchmen. Contrary to belief, there is no honor among thieves. Because they are the scum of the earth, as one Special Agent said, they will not hesitate to knife a former pal.

Men of the underworld and women, too, hate the fingerprinting records. If they could, they would blow them "higher than a kite." They may dye their hair, undergo plastic surgery to change their features, and get different dentures. But, as long as they live, they can never acquire new fingerprints.

Dillinger, the notorious bandit, once made an attempt to change his fingerprints. He would fool the G-Men, he believed!

He hired a surgeon of the underworld to remove the outer layers of the skin of his fingertips. The cost was five thousand dollars, but he considered it worth the money to be free from a fingerprint record if he were caught on his next criminal job.

He suffered miserably. For weeks his hands were bandaged and he could not use them. He could not even feed himself or pour a drink. But he chuckled as he dreamed of how he was fooling J. Edgar Hoover and his smart G-Men.

But was he? Every G-Man would like to have been present when the final bandages were removed from the fingers of the man who thought he had outwitted Nature.

At first glance the new scar tissue looked pleasantly pink and white. The fingertips looked smooth.

Dillinger held his hands under a bright electric light bulb. His yell of rage was a strangling howl. He saw, faint but clear, the very furrows and ridges he thought had been done away with. He had thought he would laugh at the G-Men, but it was the G-Men who laughed.

The notorious bad man had not known what every school child in America knows: fingerprints are never changeable!

Chapter VI

Fingerprints Protect Citizens

Everybody's fingerprints are important—everybody's! There is a fingerprint division in Washington for civilians. It has nothing at all to do with criminals. Most people think of fingerprinting and criminals as one and the same thing. But it is not the same thing. The file for the fingerprints of civilians is separate and its use is voluntary. Any person in the United States may send a copy of his fingerprints to the FBI for this file. As a matter of fact, he is urged to do so. All that is required of him is that he make application with the FBI and he will be sent a blank. Instructions will be given and he can easily prepare the simple work at home.

What good would it do for an ordinary, law-abiding person to have his fingerprints on file in Washington?

Let us consider just a few problematical cases:

A confused old woman gets off at the wrong station. She wanders about the giant concourse waiting for Cousin Hattie. For hours she sits on the hard benches, then ventures into the streets. She walks block after block, stopping people occasionally to inquire about the street address she has scribbled on a small piece of paper. She has forgotten Cousin Hattie's married name. A policeman advises her to return to the station and get in touch with the Traveler's Aid. There is no such address in the city directory. By this time the poor old soul is so upset that she cannot give a coherent account of her situation. A newspaper picture and a story finally brings a distraught Cousin Hattie to her side. . . . If she had been fingerprinted, her full name and a relative's address would have been available.

A boy riding a motorcycle hits the abutment of a bridge, his motorcycle topples over into a river, and he is rendered unconscious. At the hospital the attendants get no response in answer to their questions. It is ten days before he rallies to give them his name and address. If he had been fingerprinted, he could have been identified and his worried parents would have been notified to tell them why he had not reached his destination.

Here is another case that happens frequently: A man is found walking the streets. He has no coat or hat or billfold, yet he is well-groomed. He does not know his name or where he has come from. He knows only that he has hitch-hiked a good many miles. The city hospital is aware that this is a case of amnesia. . . . If he had been fingerprinted, he could have been identified and his wife and children would have been saved terrible worry.

Nobody should say, "I'm not going to have my

fingerprints on file with the FBI like a criminal."

J. Edgar Hoover points out that the fingerprint is the mark of one's individual self. It is an amazing miracle, for it was formed before birth and will last after death so long as the body is preserved.

In a disaster where many people are killed or injured, identification by fingerprints may solve many a mystery. Sometimes whole families are involved.

J. Edgar Hoover himself speaks out in an appeal to persuade every citizen to be fingerprinted. He says, "There is no recommendation of identity as good as that of being able to say that a citizen has thought enough of the future and of his family to place his mark of identification on file. . . . There is no stigma to such a method of identification. It is a badge of honor. It should give one a standing in a community."

A criminal would probably be the only one who would attempt to change his fingerprints. The very fact that an attempt was made, by files or surgeon's scalpels, would point to some feeling of guilt, or to some plan of criminal action.

The record cards that take impressions use both hands but only the finger tips. Below is the order:

RIGHT HAND

1. Thumb 2. Index finger 3. Middle finger 4. Ring finger 5. Little finger.

LEFT HAND

6. Thumb 7. Index finger 8. Middle finger 9. Ring finger 10. Little finger.

Then the four fingers of the left hand simultaneously.

Then the four fingers of the right hand simultaneously.

The work entails no charge and can be done anywhere, at home if the subject pleases. Instructions are simple.

Nowadays, thanks to J. Edgar Hoover, almost every business and organization realizes the value of fingerprinting. Banks demand that their personnel be fingerprinted. Hitherto, bankers have sometimes been dismayed to learn that some trusted worker had a criminal record of bank robbery or embezzlement. Police forces have discovered among their ranks men who are part of the underworld and who desire to help pals in planned crimes. The Army has found within its body men who have joined military forces for one purpose only, to hide out. Even in the Civil Service the man or woman with a criminal record could find a place were it not for fingerprinting. Many criminals are educated people, capable of passing examinations in their chosen fields.

Anyone accepting a position of trust, be it in a bank, in civil service or in military duty should not object to being fingerprinted. These fingerprints, as Mr. Hoover pointed out, are a "badge of honor."

In courts today, where both criminal and civil cases are tried, fingerprints are accepted as evidence. Projection lanterns are used to enlarge the prints to be thrown on a screen. A clear large picture will show a sameness or a difference.

A policeman or anybody else can take a fingerprint, but oftentimes a print is partially hidden on material such as paper and has become indistinct. These fingerprints are called latent fingerprints, and it takes the work of experts to make them clear. Two processes are known: the silver nitrate process and the iodine gas process. Classification must be done by experts too. To the inexpert eye the indentions and whorls all look much alike.

Methods need not concern the average citizen. The best any American boy and girl can do to help J. Edgar Hoover and the G-Men is to get his own signature on that valuable piece of paper—a registration of his fingerprints.

It is not only in America that such an identification is acceptable but in all the countries of the world. Everybody is grateful for the system for handling all these fingerprints as worked out by our own FBI.

Chapter VII

The Magical Laboratories

When J. Edgar Hoover first took over the vast job of the Federal Bureau of Investigation, he was faced with the problem of organized crime. Many honorable business concerns were threatened by organized gangs, while bootleggers were being welcomed into homes that never before had received a criminal or any other law-breaker. Gangsters, enriched with stolen loot, were hiring smart lawyers to outwit the courts. Only too often they used deceptive evidence.

The Director had his G-Men. They were hard-working, efficient, alert; and they persevered until they got their man. They were, above all, honest, and while the gangsters were amazed that they were having to deal with men who couldn't be influenced either by money or political pressure, they knew that the future would be bleak for crime. The G-Man became the bane of the criminal's existence. And soon the laboratories that J. Edgar Hoover set up were to be the bane of the crooked lawyer's existence.

The detection of crime is a scientific business, the Director decided. There can be no guess work. In setting up the finest technical laboratories possible, J. Edgar Hoover selected his workers as carefully as he had chosen his Special Agents. Every scientist had to be a specialist in his particular field. He is as important as the G-Man and he knows it. On his findings will depend the guilt or innocence of an accused person.

It was in the fall of 1932 that J. Edgar Hoover began his Technical Laboratory with one employee. Today there are over three hundred, and every single man is of good character, fine reputation, and has the kind of integrity that makes him absolutely reliable. These men are not interested in proving a man guilty; they are interested in getting at the truth. Above everything else, they want justice. It is only fitting and proper that they should be housed in the Department of Justice along with the F.B.I.

While each branch of the laboratories is separate, several may work simultaneously on a case. Suppose a man is murdered. He is shot while returning home from work in his car. The bullets extracted from the murdered man's body are sent into the ballistics department. There are bloodstains on his clothes and bits of hair and fiber in his nails, indicating that he must have struggled with his attacker. There are the tire tracks of the car that came alongside his, forcing him over to one side of the road. There are a number of footprints. Where the murderer's car jammed the victim's car, there is a scratch. In the victim's pocket is an extortion note, either pecked out on a typewriter or written in longhand.

While the bullet is being examined to learn the type or make of gun it was fired from, the hair and fibers go to other experts. The color and texture of the hair will help to reconstruct the type of individual and the fibers will tell the kind of clothes he wore. An expert can tell the make of the typewriter that wrote the note, even the age. Nor are handwriting experts fooled by attempts to change handwriting.

Hair is often the key to the facts in the case and to the identity of the criminal. First of all, the expert decides on whether the hair is human or animal, and, if animal, what animal it came from. Human hair is described by color, texture, and caliber. Is it straight, wavy, kinky, bleached, or dyed? Slides are available for the expert, showing all known animal hairs. There are also slides showing the different shades of human hair, twenty-eight in all.

A wisp of fiber will tell the color, the weave, and even the material from which a garment was made. To the casual visitor the array of instruments spread out on the gleaming tables will seem confusing. He will recognize microscopes, optical instruments and thread counters. And he will observe the collection of dyes and stains, of string and cordage, the types of weaves of various manufacturers. But intricate set-ups are for the expert.

A criminal may deny he was present at the scene of a crime. No one saw him commit the deed. But a few grains of sand from a man's shoes may prove that he was lying. How?

Soil in your own back yard may be quite different from the soil across the street. Scientists know that the rocky crust of the earth will erode into sand or soil. Under a microscope a bit of soil will look like a mass of crystals of the same composition as the parent rock from which it came. Rock varies in different localities.

Peer into the special microscope and, with the help of polarized light, see the sparkling beauty and color of the tiny grains of sand. One might think he was looking at jewels. Actually the color enables the expert to decide on the mineral source of the bit of dirt. A test is also made of the soil at the scene of the crime. If these two are identical—the soil on the shoe and the soil at the scene of the crime—then it is certain that the accused was present. He was present whether he says so or not. He may be lying, but the special microscope does not lie.

It is discovered that footprints were left in the clay or sand! This matter will be handled by another expert. First he will spray the surface of the imprint with a special substance that dries quickly but is an adhesive like shellac. In this manner the particles of sand are held in place. Now the expert can pour in, very carefully, a semi-fluid mixture of plaster that will soon harden. This model will show worn spots, patches, nails, and rubber heels. Back in the laboratory the expert may compare his model with 1800 specimens of rubber heels.

The same expert may make a print of a tire tread

and compare it with the drawings and blueprints in his office.

Other experts will have intricate instruments with which to test metals and woods. A bit of metal no bigger than a pinpoint may be found to be part of a knife a suspect carries, with which he cut a hole in a screen and through which he entered a window. A bit of paint or wood may be traced to its source to convict or free a suspect.

One less spectacular method of keeping track of criminals with a record is called "mugging." It refers simply to taking a photograph and remembering a face. It was the famous Bertillon who taught a system of memory so that having once seen a man, the police would remember him.

These are the types of faces seen in public places and marked **wanted.** The pictures are always clear, with at least two views of the head, showing the slant of the forehead, the shape of the nose, the expressions of the mouth and the details of eyebrows and ears. One may easily say, the "portrait parle" — the "picture speaks"—or that it is a speaking likeness.

Certain terms used in the laboratories contain big words with big meanings. Toxicological examinations have to do with the science of poisons. Petrography is the science of geology which deals with the identification of rocks and their minerals. Spectrography deals with small samples, such as paint.

One procedure in the FBI Identification Division is little known. This is the placing of wanted notices in fingerprint files and almost at any given time there are between 80 and 85 thousand wanted notices placed by law enforcement agencies throughout the country against persons who are fugitives from justice. In the 1963 fiscal year, FBI fingerprint examiners identified 19,541 fugitives on whom wanted notices had been placed. At the close of fiscal year 1963 there were 83,696 wanted notices outstanding.

The work was started many years ago and has been helped along by every single field office in the United States. It is no honor to be on this list of Who's Who, for every listing is a Public Enemy.

Chapter VIII

Oscar and Beulah

Any visitor who goes into the gray stone Department of Justice Building at Ninth and Pennsylvania Avenue, North West, hopes to glimpse the setting of the Chief. As he passes between the two American flags and gazes up at the FBI seal, he is aware of the serious atmosphere of the place where great problems are constantly met and disposed of.

He may well be welcomed into the office of J. Edgar Hoover. On the Chief's desk he sees another flag, a small one. This flag is always flanked by vases of fresh flowers. On the radio cabinet stands a bronze head of Dante, whose philosophy and poetry Mr. Hoover has always enjoyed. The framed pictures of mountains and deserts give one an impression of the far-flung places into which the Bureau hopes to establish law and order, an ideal way of life.

In the 30's a newspaper editor made the statement that the time had come when the United States might have to accept crime as part of the American way of life. J. Edgar Hoover did not think so. He set out to do something about it, to rid his beloved country of crime and criminals. He set out, like the modern Knight Errant he is, to do what politicians and inadequate police forces said could not be done. Nor does he think that juvenile delinquency and Communism must be accepted as part of the American way of life. He draws his sword of truth against them.

The only portrait in the office, an oil painting of Harlan F. Stone, is that of a man who also believed in an idealistic possibility. America can be made law-abiding.

Sobered by the dignity of his office visit, even though he may not meet the Chief, a visitor may brighten when asked if he would like to see Oscar and Beulah. The informal names promise something pleasant, almost gay.

Some of the visitors are fraternal acquaintances, for J. Edgar Hoover became a Mason at twenty-one. Then he went up through the York Rite to become a Knight Templar and a Shriner. Shrine charities have felt his gentle hand. He is now a 33rd degree Scottish Rite Mason.

J. Edgar Hoover's contacts, however, are not confined to any order, nor are his affections tied in with them. One of his most valued friends was the Reverend Robert S. Lloyd, a Jesuit, who was formerly head master of Georgetown Preparatory School. Father Lloyd died in 1960.

The visitor is given a description of Oscar. He is a very pale man of medium build with a receding hair-line, a rather debonair mustache, and he is usually attired in a custom-tailored conservative suit, polished shoes and an immaculate shirt and tie.

But Oscar is dead! He lies on the floor in his chaotic office, chairs and lamps overturned, the disk knocked off the open safe, file cases rifled, a gun—yes, a gun not a foot from his relaxed hand.

While the visitor turns slightly green, the attendant says, "Don't worry."

For Oscar is a dummy, albeit a life-like dead man, and he has been murdered more often than the Academy students can count. The visitor deduces a guess that this is obviously a robbery-and-murder case. But who could have committed the crime?

Special Agents move in on the scene. They discover at once that the gun lying at Oscar's hand is loaded. It could not have been used. It is evident that Oscar grabbed it out of his desk drawer to defend himself, but he was too slow. He was shot with a .38 caliber automatic, and the gun was "planted" beside him. There are heelprints on papers jerked from the files, and every piece of furniture is dusted for fingerprints, the telltale calling cards of the criminal. It is noted that Oscar had tapped his pipe out into an ash tray, half full of cigarette stubs. It is clear that Oscar must have talked quite some time with his cigarette-smoking caller—the cigarettes are noted as to brand—before he was murdered.

The mystified visitor moves on to have a look at Beulah. By this time he has some notion of what to expect—the unexpected. Beulah is an old car that has been through as many hazards as Oscar. She has been shot at, fingerprinted, examined for secret compartments containing jewels or drugs, and even her tire marks have become as familiar as her windshield.

Realism, such as Oscar and Beulah, is not designed for dramatic entertainment or to amuse visitors. It is for the sake of giving the student a vivid picture of what he may expect to handle. Quite as valuable for instruction is the wreck of a Marine Corps plane in a deep, wooded ravine near the pistol range. Here the student learns the tricks of the saboteur. To capture such a criminal, who in war or peace, has no regard for the sacredness of human life, is a duty. Every miserable, destructive method that was ever devised by a saboteur is known to the expert instructors that J. Edgar Hoover has chosen.

The damage done is never obvious, for no plane would go up if it were knowingly defective. What do students look for? An abrasive in the oil, cotton waste in a carburetor intake, a wire weakened by filing? Close on the heels of the discovery of what caused the plane to crash comes the laboratory work. J. Edgar Hoover's laboratory experts can easily trace materials used in sabotage to the exact spot in a huge industrial plant. Then it is no trick at all to find and arrest the suspect, no matter how sharp a crook he thinks he is.

Sometimes only a few hours elapse after a crash before the saboteur is picked up. He is always amazed that he could be so easily and so readily discovered. He had thought that his was the perfect crime.

The training period for the Special Agent is only

three months, but those months are always the most strenuous he has ever spent in his entire life. Most men describe it as an ordeal both physical and mental. The visitor sees only the more spectacular phases of the work, such as Oscar and Beulah, and does not realize that the new Special Agents are spending twelve hours a day in strenuous physical work, practical observation and testing, and difficult study.

These studies include courses in anti-trust violations, bank embezzlements, bankruptcy, and accounting. The Special Agent must be well informed whether he is sitting in a conference of industrial specialists or prominent bankers. His attitude must be professional and he himself must have poise and personality. In other words, he must be the kind of man that J. Edgar Hoover can proudly present from his F.B.I.

Suppose men of seemingly equal qualifications are up for consideration? What quality, Quantico is often asked, makes one man preferable to another? The men in one group may have equally good educations, have the same athletic health, and they may even look alike, as though they were "cut from the same bolt of cloth." But there's a difference.

It is the spirit of the man that J. Edgar Hoover notes. In a race horse this quality would be called "heart." And in a G-Man it can still be called "heart." It stands for cool courage; and the criminal, seeing that "look" in a man's eyes, knows that he is caught—that his career as a criminal is ended. For this G-Man is no Oscar. He is a living, breathing law-enforcing Special Agent of J. Edgar Hoover's F.B.I.

Chapter IX

No "Arm Chair" G-Man!

At the very time that Special Agents, trained by J. Edgar Hoover at Quantico, were doing the magnificent job of ridding the country of gangsters, the Chief himself was being vilified.

Success often brings foes, but the injustices of the accusations hurled against him must have rankled. However, he gave no outward sign of his honest anger. Abuse was not private. The slanderers openly expressed their unflattering opinions of the head of the Bureau.

On the Senate floor one member made the charge that the esteemed J. Edgar Hoover sat at his desk and sent out his devoted Special Agents to make arrests and to risk their lives. **He** played safe.

One day in 1936 the same senator who had criticized him sat opposite him at a committee meeting and accused him of being an "arm chair" G-Man. Friends said that J. Edgar Hoover's black eyes burned in his stern face and his jaw set. But he retained admirable composure, making no attempt to justify himself.

At that very moment a plane was warming up nearby to take him on a mission that he knew would be dangerous. He was to lead his men in an attempt to capture the gangster, Alvin Karpis. Karpis had sworn to kill J. Edgar Hoover.

He had boldly promised his pals that he would strut into the Department of Justice and shoot the man who had made it so uncomfortable for criminals.

It was purely coincidental that the Senator's unsavory remarks and the spinning propeller were in action at one and the same time. J. Edgar Hoover had been on raids before, but it had been decided by the F.B.I. to keep his presence secret on these special missions. He was never "chair-bound." As one G-Man expressed it, "He's forever bouncing about the country to make surprise check-ups on his field offices. To his Special Agents he looks like the toughest, most aggressive one of the lot—and he **is.**"

After leaving the committee that day in 1936 where he had faced the irate senator, J. Edgar Hoover got into the special plane that carried him with his men to New Orleans.

The capture of Karpis was imminent. The house in which he was hiding had been located. The G-Men closed in to wait, their guns drawn. Everybody anticipated a battle. The very air was tense.

But before the Chief was ready, Alvin Karpis walked out of the house. He came face to face with J. Edgar Hoover, the man he had vowed to kill. When the Chief reached out to grab his arm, Alvin Karpis froze to the spot. He grew deathly pale, and he looked as though he were going to faint. The sight of the vital man with the burning black eyes and set jaw was just too much for him. He strove to put on a brave front, but he was too weak. Without a word he gave up.

Someone had forgotten to bring handcuffs. They had guns, all sorts of ammunition, even tear gas—but no handcuffs. The G-Men who made the arrest had to use their neckties to bind Karpis' hands.

When another absurd incident followed, the chuckles increased. Nobody knew where the jail was. In all the plans for the capture of Karpis, there had been no thought of the whereabouts of a place to lock him up. Karpis himself offered to lead the G-Men to the jail; he had been there before. He had heard there was a new jail, but he was not sure.

But the comedy of errors ended, and the story of the capture of Karpis would become memorable in the annals of the F.B.I.

But most raids prove dangerous, and the number of men listed on the Memorial Tablet in the Department of Justice testifies to the bravery of the Special Agents who gave their lives that criminality should be erased from the national escutcheon and that lawfulness should fly its banner over the land of the free.

J. Edgar Hoover, in spite of the risks he took, seemed to bear a charmed life. His closest call came when he led his men in the capture of Harry Brunnette. A gangster pointed a pistol directly at his head. There was no chance or time to duck. The man pulled the trigger. The pistol misfired. The Chief was saved.

The Karpis incident became public knowledge. From the reaction of the people who read the news, the F.B.I. deduced the value of J. Edgar Hoover's presence during a raid. It put fear into the hearts of the gangsters and assurance into the hearts of law-abiding citizens.

The most widely known case in all F.B.I. history was the Lindbergh case. If the child of an American hero could be stolen from a well-staffed country home for ransom, no child was safe. Gangland was better organized than the government itself, and its methods of operation were even more effective. Police often worked hand in hand with these criminals and lawyers successully defended their criminal clients.

In 1934 Congress, realizing that there **was** an organization of fearless men in this country who were not influenced by politics and who could not be bought by all the gold in the coffers of the criminals, gave the F.B.I. wide authority. J. Edgar Hoover now had what he wanted to go on—not only authority but funds as well. Where interstate angles were involved, he was to be allowed to act against robbing of national banks as well as other major crimes. And these major crimes included kidnapping.

It was largely through the efforts of the F.B.I. that Bruno Hauptman was discovered as the kidnapper in the Lindbergh case. Out of the deep personal grief of the Lindbergh parents came some good, for the sympathy of the whole country demanded of Congress that the facilities to handle just such cases be enlarged. J. Edgar Hoover spared no effort.

Today at the great switchboard in the F.B.I. communications center sit operators as well trained as the Special Agents. With the help of these experts, any place in the United States can command the full help and cooperation of the Bureau—within minutes!

There is a special call, an emergency call, that may be used in such cases as that of kidnapping. It is National 8-7117. Anybody who needs help may call it.

There is no sorrow comparable with the kidnapping of a loved one, as hour after hour passes and fear for the safety of the victim reaches unendurable agony. And since no crime strikes so deeply into an American home, J. Edgar Hoover himself takes over. He becomes a tireless fighter, pouncing swiftly and ruthlessly into the desperate search.

Time is important. A minute may make the difference between life and death, for kidnappers are the most heartless of all the sordid lot of criminals. Within five minutes after a call has been received that involves kidnapping, the F.B.I. men have the roads of the area blocked and patrolled. Special police will be watching all railways, buses, and planes. Automobiles will be checked. Special agents will be in charge of all communications—telephone, telegraph, teletype, and radio,

Tips and suggestions always pour in. Some are from cranks and half-wits and some come from people who want to be helpful. Every single clue is investigated. In one case the F.B.I. followed 23,000 clues.

Since the adoption of the Lindbergh law, the F.B.I. has solved all but three cases and J. Edgar Hoover is not dropping them. The criminals involved cannot escape his stalking G-Men.

Chapter X

The Big Net of the Kidnappers

J. Edgar Hoover points out the fact that a ransom kidnapping is not an unpremeditated crime. Nor is it usually the act of a single person. Often plans have been laid months before the crime is committed and, if the ransom is to be large, it will involve a good many people, guards, hideaway attendants, go-betweens and fixers. All these people are greedy, wanting to share in the loot, and they are as guilty as the perpetrators of the crime.

In one case the F.B.I. captured twenty-one participants. All were arrested and convicted. The six leaders received life sentences, the others years in prison in proportion to their part in the crime. For under the wide authority now given the F.B.I. and the ability and persistence of the Chief and his Special Agents, it is not profitable or safe to be a kidnapper. The underworld may be dumb, but it is learning to understand that. Such was the record in the Charles F. Urschel kidnapping.

When the Oklahoma millionaire was kidnapped, the newly activated Bureau went to work—and fast!

Results were to be world-shattering for the gangster element.

The story of the kidnapping began on a July night in 1933. Mr. and Mrs. Urschel were playing cards with their old friends, Mr. and Mrs. Jarrett, on a screen porch set about with secluding shrubbery. Two men, one with a machine gun and one with an automatic, broke in and one bandit asked, "Which of you is Urschel?"

The men were silent and the bandits escorted them both to a waiting car and drove away with them.

Mrs. Urschel kept her head. She had heard the United States Attorney General in a radio address a short time before, and she went to the telephone. She asked the operator to ring National 7117.

In the meantime the bandits drove the car through the outskirts of the city where they took the men's wallets and discovered their identity. It was Charles F. Urschel they wanted. They pushed Mr. Jarrett from the car.

Special Agents arrived by train and car and plane. But it was several days before any word came from the kidnappers. Then J. G. Catlett of Tulsa, a friend of the family's, received a packet. In it was a letter asking him to act as intermediary, a letter from Charles F. Urschel to his wife, and a third letter to Mr. Kirkpatrick of Oklahoma City. Mr. Kirkpatrick was instructed to obtain the sum of two hundred thousand dollars in "genuine used Federal Reserve currency" in the denomination of $20 bills. The letter gave a warning: "IT WILL BE USELESS FOR YOU TO ATTEMPT TAKING NOTES OF SERIAL NUMBERS, MAKING UP DUMMY PACKAGES OR ANYTHING ELSE IN THE LINE OF ATTEMPTED DOUBLE CROSS. BEAR THIS IN MIND, CHARLES F. URSCHEL WILL REMAIN IN OUR CUSTODY UNTIL MONEY HAS BEEN INSPECTED AND EXCHANGED AND FURTHERMORE WILL BE AT THE SCENE OF CONTACT FOR PAY OFF."

Further instruction followed. Mr. Kirkpatrick was to advertise a farm sale daily for one week in the **Daily Oklahoman**. The ad read: FOR SALE—**160 acres land, good five room house, deep well. Also Cows, tools, tractor, Corn and Hay. $3,750.00 for quick sale— Terms. Box No.** ....

The **ad** was published as the kidnappers had ordered.

Several days passed. The kidnappers were drawing their net tighter. They must have felt that they were being very clever. A Special Delivery Air-mail letter, mailed in Joplin, Missouri, was received by Mr. Kirkpatrick. He was to pack the $200,000 in a light-colored bag. But another person was to purchase transportation and berth on the train 28, leaving Oklahoma City for Kansas City, Missouri, at 10:10 P.M.

Mr. Kirkpatrick was to ride on the observation platform. He would see a bonfire somewhere along the right-of-way, a signal preparatory to another signal of a second bonfire he would see later. Mr. Urschel would be attending the second bonfire. Then Mr. Kirkpatrick was to throw the bag with the ransom money in it from the train.

The F.B.I. made no outward move, for it would have been futile, even dangerous. The kidnappers had the upper hand so long as they held Mr. Urschel captive. Had any of the instructions been disobeyed, they would not have hesitated to kill their man. Mrs. Urschel wanted only the return of her husband.

Nobody on the train to Kansas City could have sensed anything unusual in the two men with identical Gladstone bags. But Mr. Catlett sat just inside the observation car, the bag containing the ransom money under his chair. The serial numbers had been recorded —which were not to prove "useless." Mr. Kirkpatrick's bag contained old newspapers. In case of highjacking the thieves would find no money. He sat, as instructed, on the platform. The two bonfires did not materialize.

In Kansas City the two men went to the Muhlbach Hotel according to instructions, and here they were not disappointed. A telegram arrived from Tulsa. This telegram read: OWING TO UNAVOIDABLE INCIDENT UNABLE TO KEEP APPOINTMENT ... WILL PHONE YOU ABOUT SIX. It was signed C. H. Moore.

Just before six the telephone rang and C. H. Moore was on the line. In a gruff voice he said, "This is Moore," and asked, "You got my telegram?"

Mr. Kirkpatrick replied that he had. He was then given further instructions. He was to take a taxicab to the La Salle Hotel, then walk west.

He did precisely what he was told to do. He had no choice but to obey the kidnappers whose net was being tightened. Everything was going as they had planned and they were doubtless gleeful.

He had gone west according to directions only a very short way when a stranger said to him, "I will take that bag."

Mr. Kirkpatrick handed over the ransom money.

The stranger warned him not to talk. He did say that the "title deed to the farm" would be delivered within twelve hours.

That meant that Mr. Urschel would be returned at that time.

He was returned the following day. Exhausted but clear of mind, he began to help the Special Agents that J. Edgar Hoover had assigned to the task. Now that he was safe at home, he could give the law full speed ahead.

He had been held captive for nine days, but he had not been idle. He had recorded in his mind every detail that he thought would prove valuable—seeing the brightly lighted power plant at Harrah, Oklahoma, twenty miles east of Oklahoma City . . . passing through oil fields . . . changing license plates and cars in a garage . . . the house he slept in with wads of cotton over his ears . . . the barking of a dog and the mooing of a cow, the cackle of chickens and the shrill cry of guinea hens . . . his guards . . . the second hide-out in a farmhouse . . . the battered tin cup with well water . . .

passenger planes overhead . . . more bumpy roads . . . being given a ten-dollar bill and told to walk to town, recognized as Norman, Oklahoma . . . the train to Oklahoma City and freedom!

Yes, the kidnappers had thrown out their net and had drawn in $200,000 of ransom money. So successful had they been that they had almost forgotten J. Edgar Hoover and his Special Agents.

Chapter XI

The Big Net of the F. B. I.

As soon as Charles F. Urschel had finished his detailed account of his nine-day experiences while a captive of the kidnappers, J. Edgar Hoover permitted his restive Special Agents to go into action. He held a studious conference that lasted through the night so that no time would be lost, and so that there would be no question of procedure.

It was decided, first of all, to locate the houses in which Mr. Urschel had been hidden. Those houses had to belong to the kidnappers themselves or to relatives or friends of the gangsters. To an outsider this task would seem impossible since, as one of the group said, "There are half a million houses in Oklahoma. **Find two.**"

But, for J. Edgar Hoover, it was not like looking for a needle in a haystack. Thanks to Mr. Urschel's memory and observation, the F.B.I. had certain clues to go on. The prisoner had heard planes passing overhead at 9:45 A.M. and 5:45 P.M. daily, except on July 30th when the weather was bad. Strangely enough his guards did not mind answering Mr. Urschel when he would ask, "What time is it?"

Checking the time, the number of hours, that the abductors had driven, the men estimated that the distance covered could not have been more than six hundred miles. That estimate set the territory to be covered. A check of airplane schedules helped too. What was the exact location of passenger planes passing over this area at the times Mr. Urschel heard them? The answer was: Paradise, Texas. The United States weather bureau records were consulted. It was learned that there were heavy local rains near Paradise, Texas, on July 30th.

Mrs. Kelly's parents lived in Paradise, Texas, and Mrs. Kelly was the wife of Machine-gun Kelly who was to give the Special Agents their very special name of G-Men.

The house in which Kathryn Kelly's parents, Robert Shannon and his wife lived, answered Mr. Urschel's description of the first house in which he was held prisoner. The F.B.I. gave no indication that they were on the trail. They learned that the son lived on a farm a mile and a half away. There was a deep well to the northwest of the house where the water was drawn up in a bucket suspended from a rope and pulley. It squeaked when in use. How well the Special Agents remembered Mr. Urschel's description of that squeak! And there was the dented tin cup without a handle from which the prisoner had drunk. He had mentioned the strong mineral taste of the water; the water did have a sulphuric taste. Other facts tallied—the gate, the step-up, the length of the boardwalk, the uncarpeted room, and the chair to which the prisoner had been handcuffed. It all added up.

Neighbors revealed that George and Kathryn Kelly had made a parental visit while Mr. Urschel was being held. It was decided to raid the houses.

It was daybreak. A dozen Special Agents and local police moved up around the Shannon house. At a given signal the two doors were opened and the men stepped in quietly, revolvers in hand. A Special Agent, in a preliminary investigation, had made a diagram of the house and every man knew just where to go.

In a rear room a man slept with two automatic pistols and a machine gun in bed beside him. . . . He was swiftly handcuffed. In his pockets was $700 of the ransom money. The man was the notorious bank robber, Harvey Bailey, who had escaped from the Kansas State Penitentiary.

Robert Shannon, his wife and son Armon were arrested.

Mr. Urschel identified the houses, the tin cup with the missing handle and the dents, the chair that he had sat in, the chain that had held him prisoner to the chair, and he even identified the voices of the Shannons and the son. The family whined that all they had done was to guard Mr. Urschel; they had had no part in the kidnapping. To save themselves they boldly stated that George Kelly, "Machine-gun Kelly" and Albert Bates were the guilty ones.

J. Edgar Hoover, as Director, was relieved to have Mr. Urschel safe and sound. He was also relieved to know the identity of the kidnappers. But the case was, by no means, closed. Ahead lay the task of capturing the guilty ones and their accomplices.

Immediately upon Mr. Urschel's return, Mr. Hoover had sent out the serial numbers of the ransom bills to every bank in the United States.

Results came quickly. The Hennepin State Bank of Minneapolis reported to the F.B.I. that a truck driver had deposited $1000 of the ransom bills to the account of his boss. . . . The First National Bank of Minneapolis reported a $500 deposit of ransom notes. . . . In Colorado, police picked up a vagrant with $660 of the ransom notes in his pockets. His fingerprints were air-mailed to the F.B.I. laboratories. Who should he turn out to be? None other than Albert Bates who, with "Machine-gun Kelly," had engineered the Urschel kidnapping.

On August twenty-third Albert Bates and the Shannons were indicted in Oklahoma City along with others who had shared in the loot. They had been caught by means of the ransom money serial numbers. They had learned that they could get no benefit from the money unless they spent it; and if they spent it, they were bound to be caught.

Harvey Bailey thought he could beat the law by

hacksawing his way out of prison. But his freedom was short-lived. He was caught the next day.

The Kellys covered a good many miles, striving to elude the Special Agents of the F.B.I. J. Edgar Hoover's big net would never catch **them**! Mrs. Kelly made friends with a hitchhiking couple and used their daughter as a blind. She picked up husband George in Chicago, and the three of them, looking to all the world as father, mother, and daughter, drove to Memphis, Tennessee. There George Kelly contacted a friend to get him some money that was buried on a ranch in Coleman, Texas. The friend obligingly took the child along and put her on the train to Oklahoma City so that she could rejoin her parents.

It seems almost uncanny, but this little girl's supposedly harmless chatter was what put the F.B.I. on the right trail to the Kellys. She mentioned all the fun at "Tich's" house. In the Birmingham, Alabama, field office the Special Agents made a hurried survey. In no time at all they had discovered that the home of which the child chattered was none other than that of J. C. Tichenor of Memphis.

The raid took place September twenty-sixth, two months after the kidnapping of Mr. Urschel. The squad of Special Agents and police officers surrounded the house. At a given signal heavily armed men stepped in. They stood over the sleeping couple.

"Don't make a move, Kelly," the Special Agent said in a quiet voice.

"Don't shoot, G-Man!" Kelly is said to have cried.

He and his wife were both looking into the muzzles of revolvers. They wilted. They had frightened many people, but now they were frightened.

The big net of the F.B.I. had closed them in. Life imprisonment awaited this drab couple who had thought they could forever elude J. Edgar Hoover and his G-Men.

Chapter XII

John Dillinger, Criminal

What makes a criminal? The F.B.I. will explain that wrong thinking is the basis for most wrong doing. First of all, a boy or girl thinks it smart to resist training by parents, teachers, and men of God. In the second place he does not think it necessary to respect the rights of others, and this lack, carried to extreme, may result in murder since there is no reverence for life. This second false belief is the mark of the hoodlum. The third false belief is that the wrong-doer will not necessarily be caught. He has only to read the record of J. Edgar Hoover and his F.B.I. to learn how lacking in judgment he is.

The F.B.I. is the chief bulwark against the spread of crime and Communism in this country. Law-breakers will find that they cannot ride high over all the man-made and God-made laws of the universe. It takes an egotistic fool to assume that he can be a law unto himself. Such a one was John Dillinger. He enjoyed reading such statements about himself as, "John Dillinger left a hide-out in Florida one day, robbed a bank in

Indiana the next afternoon, tucked a wounded comrade away in a hide-out apartment in Chicago the day following, and within twenty-four hours was carousing with his gang in Tucson, Arizona."

What could a modern Knight Errant mean to him? Fidelity, Bravery, Integrity were qualities he could not even comprehend. He did not fear J. Edgar Hoover or any Special Agent, not even Melvin Purvis, said to be one of the best.

John Dillinger was born in Mooresville, Indiana, June 28, 1904. There was nothing in his childhood to indicate the desperado he was to become. His father, a farmer, came of good Quaker stock. When John was three years old, his hard-working mother died. The father, probably unable to carry on the farm chores without the help of his wife, moved to Indianapolis. Here he opened a grocery store in a poor part of the town, but he did fairly well. John attended high school and played on the baseball team. On Saturdays, as many another boy has done, he helped his father in the store. With him he attended the Quaker church.

In 1920 when John was sixteen years old, the father moved back to Mooresville, probably to be near old neighbors. Again he ran a grocery store and again John helped out—but only off and on.

He had been jilted by a high school girl, and at nineteen he enlisted in the United States Navy. Six months later he deserted in Boston. It seemed that he couldn't stick to a job, neither the store nor the navy duties. A reward of $50 was offered for his apprehension, but sometime later, he was honorably discharged. To the outsider this fact may indicate that he regretted his act and was trying to make good.

The next year, on April twelfth, he married a sixteen-year-old Mooresville girl. He was twenty now, and normally he would be planning his future. Actually he spent most of his time in pool halls, associating with other idlers like himself. He did not want to work for his money. Among the ne'er-do-wells was a fellow by the name of Ed Singleton. In September, 1924, he and John Dillinger hatched a plot to rob a storekeeper by the name of Frank Morgan. The robbery was easily accomplished, for the sixty-five-year-old man made no resistance. There was no reason to injure him, but John Dillinger hit him over the head with a lead pipe.

John Dillinger was sentenced to serve from ten to twenty years in the Reformatory. Ed Singleton, who turned State's evidence, got off with a lighter sentence. Young Dillinger was furious. He hated a "squealer" and the hardened criminals he met in the Reformatory fanned his flaming hate. They told him he would be the kind of law-breaker to plan and execute the "perfect crime."

To cooperate with the authorities was farthest from his thoughts. Twice he attempted to break out and finally became so headstrong and violent that the Reformatory officials had him transferred to the Indiana State Penitentiary at Michigan City.

During the next nine years of his life he studied in this school of crime. He continued to brood about the injustices he insisted he had suffered and to urge his father to ask for a parole so that his only son could help him in his old age. People actually signed a petition to free this bitter, vengeful young man, and he was freed on May 22, 1933.

He was a parolee all right, but not an ordinary one. He laughed at the idea of helping his poor old father and set out on a perfect orgy of robberies. He had lived a frugal life in prison. Now he was going to make up for it. With his ill-gotten funds he bought rich foods and fine wines, elegant clothes and jewelry. He had his "molls."

With his perverted sense of obligation to the hoodlum friends who still remained in prison, he planned their deliverance. He knew all the tricks, he boasted, and he did get firearms into their hands. On September 26, 1933, ten of the most desperate and despicable men on record shot their way out.

In the meantime John Dillinger, after a number of bank robberies, had been arrested in Dayton, Ohio, and was then transfered to the county jail at Lima. Three of the hoodlums he had helped escape now decided they'd help him. They'd show the law what they could do.

On October 12, 1933, Makley, Clark, and Pierpont stepped boldly into the office of Sheriff Jesse Sarber to inform him that they were officers from Michigan City with orders to take Dillinger back with them. The Sheriff asked for their credentials. They drew their pistols, said, "These are our credentials," and shot him down in cold blood. They locked Mrs. Sarber and the deputy sheriff in cells, found the keys, and triumphantly took off with Dillinger.

Criminologists say that this jail delivery and murder has no rival in the history of crime.

Dillinger's gang killed wantonly and viciously. Even when their lives were not in danger, they killed unnecessarily. It is not known how many innocent people they killed. They robbed banks in Greencastle, Indiana; New Castle, Ohio; Montpelier, Indiana; Farrell, Pennsylvania; and Bluffton, Ohio, before moving on to the Middle West. They made off with several million dollars, but their killings were more terrible than their robberies.

John Dillinger himself killed Policeman William P. O'Malley when the officer attempted to arrest him during the robbery of the First National Bank in East Chicago, Indiana, on January 15, 1934. He said, "You asked for it" and shot the officer.

His escape was only temporary, for he was arrested in Tucson, Arizona, on January 22, 1934. He was taken to Crown Point, Indiana, but no one could ever explain how he escaped. He must have had confederates.

Then J. Edgar Hoover asked Inspector Samuel P. Cowley and other trusted G-Men to handle the capture. Through Anna Sage, who wanted reward money and favors to prevent her deportation, Mr. Melvin Purvis, who was Special Agent in charge of the F.B.I.'s Chicago Field Division, secured the information that, on a certain night, John Dillinger was to attend the Biograph Theatre in Chicago. Anna Sage was promised the reward money, but not the favors she sought concerning her deportation. The G-Men made their stand outside the theatre, tense but certain. An agent was to light a cigar as a signal to the other agents waiting that the man in front of him at that moment was John Dillinger. A wave of the hand was to be the signal to close in. A man came out between two women wearing dark glasses, a straw sailor, gray trousers, but no coat. The agent standing in front of the theatre struck a match, lit a cigar, and continued to stand at his post according to pre-arranged plans. Five of the agents designated as "mobile agents" moved toward the alley where Dillinger had parked his car. Three of the agents reached Dillinger just as he and the two women started up the alley toward his car. These agents said in one voice, "F.B.I. Agents—you are under arrest."

John Dillinger reached for his righthand pocket, drew his .380 automatic, but he never fired it. He dropped. He had been shot.

In his mother's home in Washington J. Edgar Hoover paced the floor, waiting. Then came the call from Special Agent Purvis. John Dillinger had ended his life of crime.

Chapter XIII

Public Rats

It was the irony of fate that Alvin Karpis should end his life of crime by coming face to face with J. Edgar Hoover himself. Nor was it surprising that the coward should wilt at the sight of the dynamic man who headed the F.B.I. But once in the car that was taking him to jail, he regained some of his egotistical arrogance.

With a sneer, he said, "Well, it took a lot of you to catch me. After all, I was Public Enemy Number One."

His voice filled with contempt, J. Edgar Hoover retorted, "You were nothing but Public Rat Number One."

Alvin Karpis could have added that he was "Ma" Barker's Number Two Man, for "Ma" Barker was also of the rat genre. The Lindbergh Law didn't bother her at all even though it warned that a victim taken across a state line would be under federal protection from the F.B.I. Nor did the tragic story of the payment of the $50,000 ransom only to find the little boy dead touch her heart. This stout, pleasant looking woman was out-wardly a motherly type; inwardly she was a tricky, malicious creature.

Who was this Alvin Karpis who was to become one of her gang and who was, inevitably, to meet up with J. Edgar Hoover and his G-Men?

He was a lazy, sullen boy even at sixteen, known for his bad temper. When the YMCA secretary tried to interest him in games, boxing, and swimming, he retorted that he was no "sissy," and, instead of getting jobs like other teen-agers in his section of Topeka, Kansas, he started breaking into candy and grocery stores, rifling cash registers. When he broke into a jewelry store, the honest pawnbroker to whom he tried to sell the stolen goods reported him to the police. Alvin Karpis was sentenced to ten years in a reform-atory for burglary but escaped at the end of two years.

He headed for Tulsa, Oklahoma, and went into "big time" crime. This was 1931, and "Doc" Barker was his idea of an arch criminal—the sort he wanted to be. "Doc" Barker had three brothers and a mother who trained her sons to be law-breakers. They became hoodlums, kidnappers, robbers, and even murderers. They cut their teeth on robberies. "Ma" Barker planned the robberies and get-aways, always careful not to break federal laws. She boasted she could handle any local police but did not care to tangle with the F.B.I. She had heard that this J. Edgar Hoover was tough.

Whether she knew it or not, the F.B.I. was aware of

her gang and its lawlessness. However, the authorities could get no evidence against her.

Into this household "Doc" Barker brought Alvin Karpis, his mother's most willing pupil. At that time she had about twenty gangsters coming and going into her headquarters. She would send them out to rob, and, if need be, kill. She had a hide-out in the Cookson Hills where she hid them while the heat was on. If they were awkward enough to get caught, after all her teaching, she hired lawyers to defend them. Her gang had committed a hundred robberies, yet "Ma" Barker had never spent a single day in jail.

Alvin was her smartest boy; he took to crime like a duck to water. Even the other gangsters looked up to him. He and "Doc" Barker robbed a store in Missouri. The car in which they made their get-away was recognized by a mechanic, and he notified Sheriff C. R. Kelly. When the Sheriff appeared to question them, they opened fire and killed him. "Ma" Barker hid her gangsters again.

But things were getting uncomfortable with police on the hunt. She moved her gang to St. Paul, Minnesota. Now she decided to kidnap some rich man and hold him for ransom. Some of the gang had seen Mr. Edward George Bremer driving his little girl to school mornings on his way to his office. It was decided to pick him up.

Their plans worked out perfectly. As Mr. Bremer stopped one morning for a traffic light, one of the gang appeared on the left side of his car, stuck a gun in his ribs, and ordered him to move over. Another gangster stepped into the car on the other side and hit Mr. Bremer on the head with a heavy instrument. He slumped to the floor as the lights changed, and the car drove on.

Promptly the next day, the ransom note was received by Walter Magee, a family friend. Even if the spelling was not perfect, the meaning was clear. The abductors demanded $200,000 in $5 and $10 bills—no new money—to be placed in two large cartons. An ad was to be placed in the Minneapolis Tribune under the personal column: "We are ready, Alice." "Ma" Barker's unsmiling pencil was evident in the context: "Don't plead poverty we know how much they have in their banks. Don't try to communecate with us we'll do the directing. . . ."

In with the ransom note was another note, this one in Edward Bremer's handwriting. Doubtless it was dictated:

"I have named you as payoff man. You are responsible for my safety. I am responsible for the full amount of the money.

(Signed) E. G. Bremer

Deal only when signature is used"

Upon receiving notification of the Bremer kidnapping, J. Edgar Hoover wasted no time. His guess was that it was the work of "Ma" Barker and her gang and that Alvin Karpis was mixed up in it. Immediately he sent out twenty extra agents to St. Paul.

Mr. Hoover agreed with the family that the ransom money should be paid.

In the meantime the kidnappers learned that the G-Men were in St. Paul, and "Ma" Barker never had liked Special Agents. It is related that when a younger son expressed doubts, "Ma" Barker said, "Don't you worry none. Your old mother is lots smarter'n the F.B.I."

Mr. Bremer now wrote Walter Magee another note to say, "The people that have me know that the police and G-Men are after them. Please call them off and work alone."

Next in the chain of events was the finding of the Bremer automobile with bloodstains on the front seat. The fears that Mr. Bremer had been killed were allayed when another note arrived, written by Mr. Bremer himself, explaining that the bloodstains were from a cut on the head and that he was all right. But again he asked that the police be kept out of the case.

After reading this note Mr. Hoover said, "We don't want to do anything that will make the kidnappers kill Edward Bremer. We'll wait until he is returned."

The expected instructions arrived. Mr. Magee was to deliver the $200,000 in ransom money by driving to Farmington, Minnesota, then following the 9:25 p.m. bus until he saw four red lights on the left side of the road. These lights were a signal to turn off on the first road to the left and drive on until he saw the headlights of a car flash five times. This meant that he was to slow his car and set the ransom money out on the right side of the road.

He followed the precise instructions. The next day Mr. Bremer was released. "Ma" Barker and her gangsters had the money and were satisfied.

Since he had been blindfolded most of the time, Mr. Bremer could report very little to the F.B.I. But he could describe the wallpaper on the room in which he slept since the blindfolds were removed nights. The G-Men procured samples of all the wallpaper that had been sold in the St. Paul area during the past few years. Mr. Bremer recalled sounds, two dogs barking, children playing, the squeal of brakes being applied (probably at a stop sign), and the sound of coal being shoveled from a bin into a cookstove. . . . With these clues the house was found—but it was empty.

However, Mr. Bremer recounted one small incident that seemed to the family to have no particular significance but was to prove valuable. He told how, after the gang had received the ransom money, they had blindfolded him again and had driven him in circles and for quite some distance so that he would not be able to locate the house again. The driver finally said that they were getting low on gas.

"The strange thing about it," Mr. Bremer reported, "was that they didn't stop at a filling station. They took cans out of the trunk rack of the car and filled the gas tank from them. Then I think they threw the tin cans away."

"If we could find these cans," Mr. Hoover reasoned, "we might find fingerprints."

For a hundred miles round about police began looking for empty gasoline cans—and found them.

Chapter XIV

One Fingerprint
Captures the Barker Gang

The sheriff of Columbia County, Wisconsin, turned over to the F.B.I. four gasoline cans and a tin funnel which had been found by a farmer near Portage, Wisconsin. When they were flown in to the laboratory in Washington, the Identification Division of the F.B.I. found only one fingerprint. But that was enough!

Within minutes J. Edgar Hoover received the report over the telephone: "The print is from the right index finger of Arthur 'Doc' Barker, one of the four sons of 'Ma' Barker."

Mr. Hoover's guess was right. The Bremer kidnapping was the work of the "Ma" Barker gang that included Alvin Karpis.

How about the four red lights on the left side of the road near Farmington that had been used as a signal? There were no such lights set out by the county to indicate danger or direction. The G-Men found four flashlights, traced them to the Grand Silver store in St. Paul, discovered the salesgirl who had sold them, and showed her several pictures. Without hesitancy she picked out one, and said with certainty, "That's the man who bought the flashlights."

The man was Alvin Karpis.

Now the Special Agents knew whom to look for. But "Ma" Barker and her gang had vanished into thin air. The hide-outs were always ready and waiting for just such emergencies.

J. Edgar Hoover was neither surprised nor dismayed. "Ma" Barker had escaped the watchful eye of the police, but the Director had something definite to work on. He had been given the numbers of the ransom bills and had sent the list to every bank in the Midwest. Some of the bills were bound to turn up. The gangsters could get no good from the money if they failed to spend it. They prided themselves on being big spenders, just as John Dillinger did. They loved luxury, good food, expensive liquor, fine clothes.

The first bills began to turn up in Chicago, Toledo, and Cleveland, not in St. Paul. The money was being spread out.

Then something happened that was to be significant. A member of "Ma" Barker's gang, "Shotgun Goetz," was found, ironically enough, dead of shotgun wounds on a street in Cicero, Illinois. To the G-Men this meant that the gang was not the loyal, solidified group it pretended to be. It was breaking up.

Like many a criminal, "Shotgun Goetz" had been unable to keep from boasting of his doubtful prowess. He had confided to one of the roomers in the boarding house that he and "Doc" Barker and Volney Davis had once picked up $200,000 in ransom money from the side of a road.

The G-Men began to look further into the life of the dead gangster. Among other interesting things, they learned that he had often visited Dr. Joseph Moran at a hotel in Chicago.

The F.B.I. knew that Dr. Moran was a plastic surgeon in gangland. His principal business was performing operations on gangsters to remove fingerprints and to change faces. The G-Men questioned hotel employees and succeeded, from descriptions and pictures, in identifying a good many of Dr. Moran's patients. Several members of "Ma" Barker's gang were included: Harry Campbell, Oliver Berg, Russell Gibson, James Wilson, and William Harrison. Chicago newspapers assisted by publishing photographs of all the known members of the gang, and the same photographs appeared in post offices all over the country captioned: "Wanted by the F.B.I."

Over and over again J. Edgar Hoover has tried to make the public see that it owes an obligation to the F.B.I. to furnish the G-Men with tips when it is possible. Crime is not the business of the F.B.I. alone, but everybody's business.

Following the publishing of the gangster pictures, tips began to come in by telephone and by mail. Certain persons were sure they had seen one of the gangsters on the street. Somebody else would insist a gangster sat near him in a movie theatre or in a restaurant. Oftentimes these tips were inaccurate, but every one was investigated, even those that seemed far-fetched.

Then, as often happens, valuable information came in. Gangsters were living in certain apartments in Chicago. When the Special Agents waited outside the apartment on Surf Street who should walk into the group but "Doc" Barker himself. With him was a woman companion by the name of Mildred Kuhlman. "Doc" did not even have time to draw his gun before he was hand-cuffed and the pair was on the way to the F.B.I. office.

Following the other tip, Special Agents went to the Pine Grove apartment and ordered all the occupants to surrender. There were four of them, and three did as they were commanded. Clare Gibson, Ruth Heidt and Bryan Bolton. Russell Gibson resisted, drew his automatic and fired at the G-Man in the doorway who returned his fire. The gangster fell dead.

In the apartment the inspecting Special Agents found a goodly assortment of firearms and a map of Florida. The town of Ocala had been circled with a pencil. Alvin Karpis and Fred Barker, the young son of "Ma" Barker who had advised her not to tangle with the F.B.I., were down in Florida. They had boasted that they were going to hunt "Old Joe," an alligator.

The G-Men did not know whether the alligator story was purely realistic or whether the two men planned to pull off a "big deal." In Ocala they learned that there really was such an alligator and that he had eluded hunters a long, long time.

They found out something even more important.

In a cottage on Lake Weir lived a young man who resembled the pictures of Fred Barker, and with him lived a woman who resembled "Ma" Barker.

Early one morning G-Men surrounded the cottage, and the inspector in charge called for those within to surrender. His answer was a blast of machine-gun fire. The G-Men fired back. The inspector urged whoever was inside to give up. Another blast of machine-gun fire answered him.

Then the ten Special Agents assigned to the task poured bullets into the place. Sudden quiet followed. When the men stepped in, they found two bodies riddled with bullets. They were the bodies of "Ma" Barker and her son Fred. In the cottage they found $14,000, part of it Bremer ransom bills.

In Miami, enjoying the luxurious life, Alvin Karpis and Harry Campbell read the stark, black headlines in the papers:

"MA" BARKER AND HER SON KILLED BY G-MEN
It certainly wasn't safe to stay in Florida. As it was, they were tired out from running here and there in fear. Had their luck run out too? Didn't the F.B.I. ever sleep?

In a second-hand car they started to drive to Atlantic City. But the F.B.I. had the number of their car. When they arrived, they were arrested, but they escaped to Quakertown where they forced a doctor to drive them to Ohio. In Toledo they met a gangster called "Burrhead" and with him planned to organize another gang every bit as good as "Ma" Barker's. The three of them robbed a mail truck in Warren, Ohio, of $72,000. Then Karpis added Sam Coker, Fred Hunter, and John Brock to his gang and they robbed a train of $34,000.

Next they did something spectacular. They flew a plane to Hot Springs, Arkansas. But the F.B.I. was hot on their trail and they had to hide out again. They chose New Orleans.

That was where Alvin Karpis came face to face with J. Edgar Hoover and almost fainted in fright. He knew that his trail of crime was ended. Life imprisonment awaited him.

J. Edgar Hoover checked on those boys in Topeka, Kansas, that the YMCA secretary had helped. Every one was a respected citizen in business or the professions. Alvin Karpis was reminded that he had had the same chance as they. He said, "I guess they were the smart ones. I was the dope."

It was that one fingerprint on an oil can that had enabled the G-Men to capture the last of the "Ma" Barker gang.

As for Dr. Moran, he was murdered by the patients he had served. Why? They said he knew too much!

Chapter XV

Dope Kings, Super-Criminals

The F.B.I. belongs to every citizen of the United States. J. Edgar Hoover's six thousand G-Men give their best and risk their lives every day of the year to protect the people of the country from hoodlums, robbers, forgers, saboteurs, and murderers. In addition they help out the Narcotics Bureau when needed.

Today there is one problem in the United States that is most serious because it is growing—the dope racket. In contrast, Scotland Yard in England can boast that it has rid itself of the dope czars. Its present problems, in contrast with ours, are comparatively small: some smuggled cigarettes of marijuana, an opium addict or two from the Orient bringing in a supply, or a drug addict who forges a doctor's prescription.

Marijuana, a weed that grows in almost any soil and whose leaf, when dried, may take the place of tobacco in cigarettes, makes for the most common problem. It is a narcotic, and, since it is luxuriant in growth especially in Mexico, it may be easily transported into the United States. However, there are places in the United States where it has been grown in vast acreages and where the Narcotics Bureau has had to stamp it out with consuming fires.

Distribution in this country of morphine, heroin and marijuana, has been handled by syndicates with the work done by dope peddlers. If they confined themselves to dope addicts, their nefarious business would not grow to any dangerous dimensions. But they peddle their wares to school children and to teen-agers.

There have been dope traffickers whose business was so extensive that they called themselves kings. Actually they were super-criminals who harmed their victims physically, morally, and spiritually.

Such a person was Waxey Gordon. His police record began in 1915 when he was twelve. Before he was through, he had served prison sentences in Leavenworth, Sing-sing, and the Tombs.

During the Prohibition era he became a bootleg baron, and he prospered to an amazing extent. He owned several breweries within a short distance of New York City, and he pumped beer into bottling and barreling plants set up in garages. How? He used the sewers! By means of pressure hose run secretly through the sewer pipes, he sent hundreds of thousands of gallons on its way. People drinking illicit beer in speak-easies probably never knew that it had been run through the sewers.

Somehow Waxey Gordon managed to stay out of

jail. There were other bootleg barons, and the police and public were apathetic. Then, in 1933, Thomas E. Dewey won a conviction against Waxey, not on boot-legging but on evasion of income tax, and the bootleg king—or baron, as many called him—served seven-and-a-half years out of his ten-year sentence. He signed a pauper's oath to save himself paying his just debts to the government.

A year later, in San Francisco he was picked up as a vagrant and sent back to New York where he fought to stay—and did. He was later arrested for black-mar-ket handling of sugar, served a year's time, then was arrested for receiving $40,000 worth of stolen watches, but was freed. He ran a bar and restaurant for awhile, but his license was revoked.

He was living in great luxury with no obvious source of income. The Federal men became curious especially when rumors reached them that Waxey was dealing in narcotics on a large scale. He was seen associating with racketeers on the West Coast, but there were not enough narcotic agents to follow him day and night with the hope of catching him "with the goods on." The Narcotics Bureau was understaffed and a man could not be arrested because of rumors.

But here the F.B.I. was of assistance. It is very seldom that a top dope racketeer is an addict. He seldom takes dope because he knows what it does to the user. But Waxey Gordon was himself an addict, and the Special Agents knew that he would be bound to give himself away. They guessed right. On two occa-sions he sold heroin to under-cover agents and did not realize that he was accepting marked notes in payment.

His friends tried to bribe the agents to let Waxey go, and Waxey himself, down on his knees to the Detective Sergeant of the New York Narcotics Squad pleaded, "Please kill me, John; shoot me. I'm an old man and I'm through. Let me run, John; then shoot me."

He found the thought of being in prison without drugs unbearable torture. Yet he had sold to countless others through his peddlers. He had seen men and women so bedeviled by the craving for drugs that they would steal or even murder to get money for themselves.

Twenty-three others were rounded up with Waxey Gordon, and the dope kings tottered off their thrones. The man who had made a fortune pumping beer through the city sewers was through. People who knew him well said that where he belonged was in the sewers.

It is difficult to estimate how many crimes have been committed because of drunkenness and dope. J. Edgar Hoover once solemnly wrote, "Within the space of a lifetime one hundred million Americans can look forward to the unpleasant experience of becoming victims of crime. The nation can expect to pay—in tribute to the lawless—more each year than it costs to maintain all our educational institutions. During the next generation more Americans will be murdered than lost their lives from enemy fire in World War II."

He urged that the full force of public opinion be thrown on the side of justice.

The statement sounds exaggerated until one reads actual figures.

Serious offenses in 1962 were estimated at 2,048,-370. For every day in 1962 an estimated 23 persons were feloniously slain, and 382 other felonious assaults were committed. Forty-five rapes occurred, 1,479 larcenies (over $50) were recorded, 976 cars were stolen and there were 261 robberies and 2,446 burglaries.

And here are the heart-rending statistics that touch the troubled parents, teachers, and church workers of the day. This is still the 1962 report. Reports for the country as a whole showed that juveniles (under 18) accounted for 62 per cent of the arrests for car thefts. They also figured in 49 per cent of the burglary arrests and 51 per cent of the larceny arrests. Greedy desire for someone else's possessions may be a main cause, but when mixed with dope it adds to the flame of criminal intent.

England's Criminal Investigation Department, familiarly known as Scotland Yard, admires without stint the F.B.I. in the United States. The C.I.D. is aware of the limited powers of the F.B.I. The F.B.I. can assist in investigating a crime only when that crime violates federal law. However, it serves all law-enforcing agents: it does analysis, research, and makes a study of evidence, giving testimony in courts.

Scotland Yard looks askance at the United States where, in 1952, 215,310 automobiles were stolen. In England the figure was 746. One must consider, Americans retort, that there are more cars in America, more parking places, and more opportunity. The British experts ask whether or not dope may have something to do with the thieving. They are shocked over our growing dope problem.

True, the dope kings prospered in this country before the G-Men and the agents from the Federal Bureau of Narcotics ran them down.

Take the case of "Little Augie." He was an Italian dope handler in New York who made friends with smugglers and Chinese agents to get the narcotics for him. In Istanbul he did business with the world king, Abow Isaac. The two of them could hardly believe it when they were picked up by American agents who had followed them all over Europe and arrested them in Berlin.

"Old Isaac" had double-crossed "Little Augie." "Little Augie" never suspected the old man. He had seen the heroin packed into drive shafts and cylinders of machinery to be shipped to him in America. As a matter of fact, the shipment had rumbled off to the warehouse as "Little Augie" paid his bill. Then "Old Isaac" hired thieves to steal back the heroin packed so carefully into the machinery and the machinery would arrive in America without a trace of heroin. Then the wily dealer wired "Little Augie" a message in code that he had another lot of heroin that he would ship as face powder. Gladly "Little Augie" bought it, never dreaming that he was buying the same drug twice.

When the two biggest international drug kings

were arrested and tried, "Little Augie" was more incensed by the trick played on him than by actually being taken into custody.

He said he hoped "Old Isaac" would get life imprisonment and that he would live a hundred years.

Such was the honor and affection between the two dope kings who thought they could control the world market in narcotics.

"Little Augie" got two years in prison and a $4,000 fine. But "Old Isaac" did get life imprisonment in a German jail.

Chapter XVI

J. Edgar Hoover's Homes

As a small boy J. Edgar Hoover often played near Rock Creek in northwest Washington with friends of his own age, hunting wild flowers, watching birds, and playing ball. But home was back on Seward Square, the gray stucco house with its shining windows and handsome curtains. It was the kind of home that represents the best in the American tradition: the father an honest, hardworking public servant, 'the mother a kindly, understanding woman, the children congenial. Dickerson, or Dick as he was called, took a comrade's delight in the vigorous young J. Edgar that he had once wheeled in a babybuggy. Lillian was proud of her little brother and much concerned for his welfare.

Later Dick and Lillian moved away and married, although Lillian was to return to Washington as a widowed invalid. She was Lillian Hoover Robinette, known as a woman of great charm.

J. Edgar, however, was to make his home on Seward Square in the same house for forty-five years.

It was here that the two brothers made their idealistic plans to become ministers. The inspiration of Dr. Donald Campbell McLeod was doubtless responsible for their decision. However, they faced reality and decided that, after all, they were not "cut out" for the purely religious life.

J. Edgar Hoover's study of law was certainly not designed to place him in the Justice Department. When he first entered the Department of Justice, he thought it only temporary. Later on, he planned to go into the practice of law. Of course he never did.

When "Mother" Hoover died in February, 1938, the house on Seward Square ceased to be a treasured home. J. Edgar's mother had been his companion, his adviser, and his invaluable hostess, welcoming the new Special Agents that her son brought home, making them feel valued and wanted.

The beauty of Rock Creek must have stayed in the mind of the boy all through the years, for after his mother's death, he bought a home there. The large brick house is located on the edge of Rock Creek, quite a fashionable location. It is a sturdy, solid-looking house, as substantial as the man who lives in it. There are naturally no frills; and the owner is proud of his lawn. Sometimes, when life is not too hectic, he putters about the place like any other home owner.

J. Edgar Hoover, man of many abilities, has one weak spot: he is no agriculturist. Nor is he apt to be taken in by cheats or people who misrepresent their wares—he has a pride about such things. However, on an afternoon of a pleasant day, proof became apparent that Mr. Hoover was only human after all.

A farmer stopped his truck to watch J. Edgar Hoover working on his lawn and called out, "That lawn needs fertilizer, Mister."

"Yes, I guess it does," Mr. Hoover agreed.

The farmer said he had just what the lawn needed and sold Mr. Hoover a half load of "sheep manure" for $30. J. Edgar carefully spread the newly bought "fertilizer" over the greening grass and wetted it down with a sprinkler. His two Cairn terriers, Butch (now dead) and G-boy, romped joyfully about. The dogs wore District of Columbia dog tags numbers 3 and 4, and, being high in the canine social strata, actually sensed the expectancy in the air. This would be the finest, greenest lawn in the Rock Creek district. The housekeeper rejoiced to see Mr. Hoover so interested in beautifying his yard.

Mr. Hoover's satisfaction was short-lived. When his best friend, Clyde A. Tolson, came to look over the improvement J. Edgar has boasted about, he looked more worried than usual. Then, even more unusual for him, he burst into uncontrolled laughter. Mr. Tolson did know quite a bit about barnyard products.

"Your 'sheep manure' is nothing but sawdust and dirt," he explained.

He might have added that he bet this was the only time anybody had ever put anything over on J. Edgar Hoover.

Washingtonians know about Clyde A. Tolson, not only as J. Edgar Hoover's associate director, but as his constant companion. The men are almost inseparable, and they represent a striking contrast. Mr. Tolson is as somber as Mr. Hoover is effervescent. A newspaper man once said, "Even when he feels good, Tolson looks worried."

Because of the strenuous life he must lead, J. Edgar Hoover maintains what his friends call "a strictly fenced-in" private life. That does not mean that he is not hospitable, even gregarious, but he does not go in for many social affairs. He often invites close friends in to dine or takes them out to famous restaurants. He is seen most frequently with Clyde A. Tolson in their favorite restaurant, Harvey's, and the chef says they usually order chops or steaks. Like most people in this country, J. Edgar Hoover enjoys hamburgers and Angel Food cake.

And like many of his countrymen he loads his house with antiques. His choice pieces are bronze.

For relaxation he sees a movie, watches the Washington Senators play baseball on TV, or goes to a night club when he is in New York. During the Maryland racing season, he gets to the tracks occasionally. He once played a fast game of tennis but now puts in that extra leisure fishing or taking long walks. He does everything with vigor: he walks fast, talks fast, and thinks fast. Like his Special Agents he is a good pistol shot and visits the range at Quantico periodically.

When he is in Washington he attends church regularly and seldom misses services when on trips. The teachings of his childhood are still part of his adult life, grace at meals, church attendance, and Bible reading. Today he attends the National Presbyterian Church in the capital, the same church that President Eisenhower attended.

His pastor, Dr. Edward L. R. Elson, says of his distinguished member, "His most cherished possessions are the finger-worn Scriptures of his mother and the New Testament he won for Bible memory work."

Although he is a bachelor, he has an almost paternal concern for the welfare of young people. He devotes valuable time to boys' organizations. He is a trustee of George Washington University and a member of the Board of Directors of the Boys' Clubs of America.

The Knights of the Round Table, following King Arthur into danger, had no finer **esprit de corps** than the F.B.I. working with J. Edgar Hoover. The British police of Scotland Yard cannot withhold their admiration for our Bureau. One of them said, speaking of the motto on the Bureau's crest—Fidelity, Bravery, Integrity: "Agents live and die for that motto."

One tragic incident illustrates this truth. A Special Agent, in a gun battle with two bank robbers, was fatally wounded. He lived long enough only to identify the bandits, and his last words were, "Tell Mr. Hoover I did my best."

J. Edgar Hoover himself resolutely denies that he is the sole inspiration for his men. He assures the country that there will always be men of honor will-ing to take the places of those who go into other busi-nesses or retire—or who die in the performance of their always-dangerous work. The Chief with his locked brief case, reported at the Department of Jus-tice, is no exception. But he walks bravely and confi-dently forward, his sword of justice drawn against law-lessness.

Chapter XVII

The Bad Money of
Counterfeiters and Forgers

No man is an island, it is said, and even so great a man as J. Edgar Hoover cannot handle, even with his Special Agents, all phases of crime within our country and abroad. That is where the T-men come in along with Interpol.

J. Edgar Hoover's F.B.I. men operate in the Department of Justice while the Secret Service men, who are also G-men, operate in the Treasury Department. They have two distinct duties. One is to act as a personal bodyguard to the President of the United States. Any picture of our President riding in a public parade, for instance, will show the alert men who guard him. The other duty is to care for our money.

These men, like J. Edgar Hoover's Special Agents, are expertly trained. Like Mr. Hoover's men, they must be physically fit, able to use firearms, and willing to go anywhere at any time. They take care of our money, but they may be sent to any foreign country at any time, to trail a counterfeiter, or to apprehend a traveler passing bogus bills.

Counterfeit money is the best known of all counterfeiting attempts but the easiest to detect. However, there are other forms of counterfeiting that involve millions of dollars. Counterfeit revenue stamps are pasted on bottles of illicit liquor, thus robbing the government of its high federal tax.

Americans are making trips nowadays as never before, and the opportunity looms large in the printing of travelers' checks. This racket is an international one. It was learned in recent years that the checks were printed in Spain and Portugal to a great extent. Travelers' checks represent actual money and are easy to cash. Tourists especially carry them instead of any great amount of cash. Besides, the exchange in foreign money is always carefully worked out on these checks. It would not prove difficult for the average forger to copy the handwriting of the one who possessed the check.

Not so long ago there was so much of this "money" on the market, both here and abroad, that police chiefs and bankers attended a conference of Interpol.

What is Interpol? It is the International Commission of Criminal Police. Where international bankers are concerned, it assists the C.I.D. in Great Britain and the F.B.I. in the United States.

It meets once a year and is made up of representatives of every country except Russia. It is hoped that Russia also will join this always harmonious organization. Its president was the former head of the Belgian Surete and its secretary comes from France.

Interpol keeps records of all known international criminals. The members exchange information regarding new discoveries in police science, in methods of investigation, and in detection of deception.

Just as J. Edgar Hoover makes available the use of his laboratories, so Interpol makes available its services.

Its present aims were stated by the Secretary-General at the Rome Conference in 1954.

He said, "The ideal state of affairs will come about when the sole function of the police is to prevent crime. That has not yet come about. It is, therefore, necessary to seek a balance between the preventive and suppressive duties of the police in safeguarding society. Interpol has, for many years, studied problems relating to the prevention of crime and has been encouraged to do so by various organizations in the United States."

At this meeting close contact with social questions was recommended, and it was advised that a special study be made of juvenile delinquents.

One unusual job of counterfeiting is that of printing Irish Sweepstakes tickets. It is a ticklish thing to handle. The sale of Irish Sweepstakes, to begin with, is illegal. So is the distribution. The problem of dealing with the counterfeiting of tickets already illegal presents a difficult legal question.

Counterfeiting is handled by the T-men or Treasury-men.

Such a case arose in 1951 when great quantities of counterfeit money and dope were flooding the market. It took the combined efforts of the T-men, the Narcotics Bureau, the Immigration Service and the F.B.I. to catch the crooks. Working together has always proved effective. It was the F.B.I joining in with the C.I.D. that discovered the leaders of the travelers' check racket.

The counterfeit money and dope racket revolved around one Joseph Orsini, arrested for illegal entry into the United States by immigration officers. He had escaped from a French jail where he was serving a sentence for fraud. Then it was discovered that Orsini was, with help, directing a dope-smuggling racket and carrying on, at the same time, a lively business in counterfeit money.

The Federal Agents permitted him to go ahead with his nefarious businesses until they were satisfied that they could catch the entire ring. On July 28, 1951, they made raids simultaneously over the entire country. The Orsini Ring had smuggled in around thirty million dollars in dope in two years and had peddled another million dollars in bogus notes.

The average citizen thinks of the making or mutilating of coins as a major counterfeiting job. But it takes craftsmen to make coins and the value is never great enough to face the risks. One of the most spectacular and pressing problems that Interpol ever faced was gold smuggling from India. J. Edgar Hoover assisted in these cases along with Scotland Yard.

Both Interpol and C.I.D. admire the way in which problems of forgeries are ironed out in the F.B.I. laboratories. Codes and secret writing have their place in this department with the identification of handwriting. A forger may attempt to change his penmanship by scribbling, writing with the left hand, slanting or backhand attempts or even block-printing. To the experts a person's characteristics show up in his writing as clearly as his fingerprints.

One of the most interesting cases that ever came to the attention of the G-men was that of Harry Mills, because he was not essentially a criminal. He was, to begin with, a competent engraver out of work.

During the depression he had lost his job in New York. He was let out when the force was cut down, not because of his lack of ability but because of his drinking which made him unreliable. He returned to Providence, Rhode Island, his home town, but failed to land a job. In his enforced leisure he did a little engraving, copying some fine products of the engraver's art of the Bureau of Engraving and Printing in Washington. His first duplicate was an Indian head that he used on a card to introduce himself to possible employers. No jobs were open.

He continued to practice, and he was etching a plate of one of the Hamilton ten-dollar Federal Reserve Bank Notes when he was forced to move to a cheap room in Brooklyn near the Navy Yard.

In a saloon there he met Sam De Santi and boasted

to him that he could duplicate any piece of currency. He showed him some of his work. Eventually he got into the toils of a gang that used his talents to print counterfeit bills. He could not get free.

And so Harry Mills, who had no criminal record to begin with, used his fine ability to try to beat the government. While serving his jail sentence he learned, what he should have known all along, that crime does not pay.

Chapter XVIII

Assigned to Find Spies and Traitors

It was in 1939 that President Franklin D. Roosevelt informed J. Edgar Hoover, as Director of the F.B.I., that the F.B.I. was to act as "the central clearing house of all law-enforcement bodies." All reports relating to espionage, counter-espionage, sabotage, subversive activities, and neutrality violations were to be sent to Mr. Hoover.

Under J. Edgar Hoover's direction the F.B.I. had already done a great deal of work in handling cases of sabotage, but much of it had to be kept secret. The public thought of the G-men as gang-busters. But J. Edgar Hoover had set for himself the huge task of getting information on the espionage groups being formed in the United States. Valuable also was his list of subversives.

A group of German spies, thirty-three in all, were arrested in June, 1941, prior to Pearl Harbor. Sentences were light because we were not at war. Espionage in peace-time is quite different from espionage in war-time.

Then came the very serious case of espionage of Oberleutnant Hans Peter Krug and Max Stephan's treason. The facts for the trial were furnished by the F.B.I. Krug was a Nazi who had escaped from a P.O.W. camp in Canada and who was given shelter and help by a Pro-German American, Max Stephan. There were many ramifications in the situation, but finally Krug was returned to Canada and Stephan was sentenced to hang. However, the President commuted the sentence to life imprisonment. That treason is a despicable crime was made plain to the German Bundist groups and to all German sympathizers in the United States.

Just as dangerous to the safety of our country was the case of the "doll woman" who engaged in espionage for the Japanese. She was a tiny, middle-aged woman who ran a doll shop in New York City. A letter received in what appeared to be a seeming jumble about dolls was turned over to the postal authorities and then to the F.B.I. Only an F.B.I. cryptographer could deduce from the curious letter the facts that had nothing to do with the doll business of Velvalee Dickenson. The experts reported that it was in open code. It dealt with the location, condition, damage and repair of various naval vessels of the United States.

The reference to the "new dolls" was interpreted as referring to warships recently in the Pacific. Who but one of J. Edgar Hoover's experts could guess that a description of odd character dolls could be significant? "An old fisherman with a net over his back" indicated an aircraft carrier (which is draped with safety nets). "An old woman with wood on her back" meant a warship with a wooden superstructure. "A little boy" doll was a destroyer. A Mr. Shaw referred to in the letter stood for the U.S.S. Shaw, a destroyer whose bow had been bombed away at Pearl Harbor and had been re-built in Honolulu.

Then Mr. Hoover's typing experts began studying the five letters in their possession, all about dolls. The fact that they had been typed on different machines did not dismay them. Every person has a different touch and can be identified by a distinct unevenness in pace and pressure. It was apparent that the letters were all typed by the same person even though they came from different cities and were written on various typewriters (probably rented).

Another fact of interest to the F.B.I. was that Velvalee Dickenson seemed to have plenty of money even though her doll shop could scarcely have paid expenses, and she herself was paying most of her bills in cash in $100 denominations. Four of her notes were traced to Japanese official sources that had received the money before the war, between July 25th and Pearl Harbor. But where was Velvalee keeping her hoard? The F.B.I. kept trailing her, and the day came when a couple of G-men stood beside her as she opened her safety deposit box. They reported that the sweet, mild little woman scratched and fought like a cat when they arrested her.

On trial she blamed everything on her deceased husband, maintaining that the letters were dictated and that she really didn't know the significance of any of the references. She did admit that her husband had received about $25,000 from the Japanese in return for the information he was able to turn over to them. The judge gave the doll woman ten years' imprisonment and a $10,000 fine.

But the most shocking case that ever came to the F.B.I. was the case of a physicist turned traitor. When J. Edgar Hoover learned that important atomic bomb secrets had been stolen and delivered to Russia, he turned pale, associates said, and looked stunned.

This man, who had faced every sort of criminality, could scarcely believe this. Yet, in front of him on his desk was absolute proof, true information. He would never reveal the informer.

J. Edgar Hoover called in his top men. Never had there been a more important conference. Who had given the atomic bomb secrets to Russia? WHO?

No outsider could have gotten into the big atomic plants at Oak Ridge or at Los Alamos. They were too well guarded. There was only one possibility. Some scientist—and he had to be a great physicist and mathematician even to understand the formulas—had made copies of the secret information and had passed it on.

WHO? The F.B.I. men eliminated, first of all, the Italian and Swedish scientists who had lived in their adopted country many years and had given unstintingly of their services. The British scientists, vouched for by their government, were also checked off.

Next came the name of Dr. Klaus Fuchs, German born, the son of a Lutheran minister. He had fled to

England because of his hatred of the Nazis. At Harwell, England's atomic research plant, he had been regarded as a great physicist, as indeed he was. In 1943 he came to the United States with others to work on the atomic bomb. He stayed until 1946. Now, in 1947, he was back at Harwell.

Mr. Hoover instructed his F.B.I. men to look into Fuchs' life. This tall, stooped man with thin hair and a shy manner seemed typical of the men that are absorbed in science. Most of the American atomic scientists spent their evenings together, talking over their problems, but Fuchs would leave at closing time.

Sometimes he would ask for a leave of two or three days. Occasionally he had late night visitors at his rooming place.

Mr. Hoover was given other clues, not to be made public, and he decided that Klaus Fuchs was the only man who could have committed what the Director called "The Crime of the Century."

The British Secret Service was as shocked as J. Edgar Hoover had been. Fuchs was one of the world's greatest experts on the atomic bomb.

The British arrested Dr. Klaus Fuchs who broke down and confessed the enormity of his crime. Before Hitler came into power, he had been a Communist, and he had given the secrets of the atom bomb to the Russians. Who was the agent? He did not know, only that he was a man who would pass unnoticed in a crowd, and that this man was an American chemist.

Fuchs seemed horror-stricken at what he had done and he told the British agents everything.

Where to find the American chemist who had sent the secrets to Russia!

J. Edgar Hoover said, "This is the greatest challenge the F.B.I. has ever been asked to meet. This man is the link between our atomic research program and Moscow. Even while we talk, he may be receiving still more secrets from other traitorous scientists and passing them on to Moscow."

The F.B.I. Special Agent on the case ran down Harry Gold who admitted that he was a Communist Agent and America's first atom bomb spy. He admitted that the F.B.I. had been more than fair and that his fair trial could not have happened in Russia. He said, "I can never express to you, Judge, nor to anyone else, how deep and horrible is the remorse I feel for my traitorous conduct."

J. Edgar Hoover thanked the agent who had stayed valiantly on the case even when the solution seemed impossible. Harry Gold had seemed so frank, so innocent, so loyal.

Mr. Hoover said gravely, "We don't give medals to our men."

"We don't need them, Mr. Hoover," the agent said with a smile.

Always it is enough for the F.B.I. to serve.

Chapter XIX

Communism Threatens Our Country

No knight in the Middle Ages or in legend ever faced so dangerous and insidious an enemy as J. Edgar Hoover, a modern Knight Errant, faces in Communism. Every American should look on Communism as it actually exists, for it is a monster. He should ask himself whether or not he would like to live under Communist rule. Rather, he should ask himself whether or not he would be able to endure life under a dictatorship.

Mr. Hoover probably knows more about Communism than any other man. He gives a vivid picture to Americans with the hope that they will look closely at it. One thing would not need to worry the typical American—whom to vote for. He would have nothing to say regarding any candidate for election, city, county, state, or national.

The United States would be ruled by about twenty men. This open dictatorship would be called the "dictatorship of the proletariat" and it would be carried out by force. Any or all trials held would be simply for the purpose of carrying out the decisions of the leaders.

There would probably be no Washington, D. C. One plan suggests that the capitol be located in some industrial city, like Chicago.

The Constitution of the United States, that we so dearly prize, would be abolished. Local governments would be no more, for there would be no need of a mayor, a chief of police, or a councilman.

Churches might not be done away with at first, but they would be severely taxed. Clergymen and priests would be disposed of since the new government would have no place in its plan for religion. The Communist says, "There is no God. God does not exist. Why go to church? Why worship Him?"

Along this same line of thinking is the idea that any sort of religious instruction is folly. All religious schools would be forbidden.

Certainly never would such a set-up as the F.B.I. be permitted. J. Edgar Hoover has affirmed time and time again that the F.B.I. is no Gestapo and that we can never accept a Police State. The honest investigation that J. Edgar Hoover employs through his Special Agents would be replaced by the crude and cruel methods of the secret police, the dreaded "Red Guards." Even the people of Russia fear them and their methods. And there are probably many people in Russia who have a firm religious belief and long to express it. It is to be fervently hoped that in time the Russian people will do away with Communism and be converted to a true democracy. J. Edgar Hoover makes such an attempt in his book, "Masters of Deceit." The sad fact is that very few Russians ever see this revealing book. They are not allowed to read what they please.

In a Communist State all property is owned by the State. Since this is the case, all property owned by any individual is confiscated. It is hard to understand that homes, businesses, bank deposits and even personal possessions belong to **everybody.** The leaders, as has been observed, get the lion's share.

In a Communist State, Mr. Hoover emphasizes, all industry is nationalized. That means that factories, plants, stores, and shops come under the management of the dictatorship. Workers receive wages set by the dictators, and the hours too are determined. Naturally no laborer would be permitted to organize a union nor would he be permitted to strike. Shorter hours, more pay, and better working conditions? These things are not an individual matter; there is no personal freedom.

Farms would be taken away from the farmers, but they might be allowed to work on their own land. However, they could not sell their produce or keep any of the fruits of their labor. And most certainly they would not be allowed to sell any of the land or a parcel of it. It is not **theirs.** It belongs to **everybody.**

The "Red Guard" would enforce orders. If a citizen refused to obey, he would be imprisoned, exiled to a concentration camp, or summarily shot. The Proletariat would tell every citizen where he is to live, what he is to be paid, what he is to think, and how he is to educate his children. If one has a large house, he must take in others. Perhaps a number of people must live in one room. For most Americans this way of life is unthinkable.

Americans have always felt so safe that it is hard to realize that an enemy, bigger and more deadly than any legendary dragon, waits to pounce. For that is the aim of the Communist party, to overthrow the United States government by infiltration or by force.

Many laugh at the idea. There will always be parties, they say, even crackpot parties. Anyway, according to Party officials, there are only 10,000 members in the Communist Party in the United States. What they do not know is that there is an underground of Communist sympathizers and agents ready to obey the dictates of Moscow.

Could a small group of saboteurs cripple a big American city, for example? It could. How?

J. Edgar Hoover explains. Agents would be planted in key positions in power plants, telephone and telegraph and transportation companies. At a given signal the power system of the city could be wrecked. Electricity cut off, all lights would go out, subways would be halted on their tracks, and traffic signals would fail. Mr. Hoover then points out how easy it would be for a group of Communists, using Commando tactics, to invade the National Guard armories where they would find enough ammunition to arm five thousand hoodlums. The millions of workers pouring out of offices and factories would be helpless. It is easy enough to imagine the panic.

It couldn't happen? It's too fantastic? There are no such plans? The plans of the Communists are not secret to Mr. Hoover or his F.B.I.

A short time ago an F.B.I. agent was shown a small, paper-backed booklet titled, "Official Regulations of the Game of Football." He started to read it, only to discover that it had nothing at all to do with football. It was an informative booklet on sabotage, how to destroy installations such as high tension electrical lines, central electric plants, city reservoirs and water systems. In other words, the writer was showing how to cripple a city.

Mr. Hoover's men then looked into the other innocent-appearing booklets on sports, baseball, hockey, and softball. These booklets gave instructions on how to kill off the important men in a community, how to disguise time bombs, and how to short-circuit electric power to cripple industrial plants. These were certainly how-to-do booklets. They were published in Spanish.

Obviously such booklets could not be sold on the open market. How did they get into the hands of the F.B.I.? A seaman had been ordered to throw some damaged goods overboard. He thought that possibly the sardines were not spoiled and pried a can open. The can did not contain sardines, but thirty-three booklets containing complete rules and instructions of sabotage methods. The seaman turned the booklets over to the F.B.I., grateful that he had been lucky enough to keep the information from falling into the hands of people bent on destroying whole cities.

Communists in this country maintain that they are only another political party. They say, "We are just like the Democrat and Republican parties."

But J. Edgar Hoover comes back at them with this statement, made to a United States Senate Committee, "The Communist Party is not a real political party. It is a highly organized, militant, and disciplined group of conspirators which follows the dictates of international Communism."

Mr. Hoover went on to prove again that the real aim of the Communist Party was to overthrow the United States government, by force.

The Communists always carry American flags in their parades. These flags are mere camouflage. They do not mean what the Stars and Stripes mean to Americans who pledge allegiance to that flag which stands for liberty and justice to all.

Unlike the Communists almost all honest Americans affirm their deep faith as they say "under God."

Note: Bishop Fulton J. Sheen, in a newspaper column, says: "Communism always boasts that it loves the poor and it hates the rich. But it loves the poor to make them instruments of violence in the forcible confiscation of wealth. Every Communist has capitalism in his soul and poverty in his pockets. He is rich in his avarice, poor for the moment in his possessions. But once the rich are dispossessed, he becomes more avaricious than any capitalist."

Chapter XX

One Set of Values for Juveniles

Close to the Centennial Train on the State Fair Grounds of St. Paul, Minnesota, on Labor Day in 1958 stood a large truck designated as the Crime Prevention Caravan. It was sponsored by the Chief of Police Association and the Juvenile Officers' Association, and its purpose was to bring to the public some idea of the problems law-enforcing officers face with juvenile delinquents. They maintain that 97 per cent of children under eighteen are law-abiding and that only three per cent are delinquent. But just as one rotten apple may spoil a whole barrel, just so three per cent of delinquents may spoil a whole community. The trend is not encouraging, for more teen-agers were arrested this year than last. Destruction of school and public property was greater.

Minnesota Statutes define a juvenile delinquent as a child who violates State laws or City ordinances, is habitually truant from school, is incorrigible, associates with vicious or immoral persons, runs away from home, frequents any place which by his presence is a violation of the law, habitually uses obscene, profane, or indecent language, and is guilty of lewd or immoral conduct involving another person.

These references to delinquency are mild compared to the gangster tactics of the many young criminals of today, for it is a fact that, out of delinquency, comes crime. The wrong-doing is a matter of degree.

The Caravan displayed zip guns and home-made types taken away from teen-agers and knives that had been used in fights and in cutting movie and bus seats. These knives might have been used, to good advantage, in woodcarving and cabinet making.

Gruesome pictures depicted the results of careless driving, and equally sordid photographs exhibited the awful penalty of becoming a narcotics addict.

A tour of Minnesota was planned to plant seeds of respect for law. One older officer observed that a generation or more ago, there was discipline in the home and children were not coddled. They had chores to do and were held responsible for their actions. Today, he said, mothers do not want their precious youngsters inhibited, and fathers are too busy with their own interests to check on the children's activities, good or bad. J. Edgar Hoover has expressed just this situation in the statement, "We have tried the practice of overindulgence, and it has failed. In the interest of self-preservation it now is time for sterner measures."

Character, Mr. Hoover has always maintained, begins in the home. We might add that it cannot begin too early. Mothers sometimes say, "I know he's a brat, but wait until he gets into school. The teachers'll take it out of him." Or "Wait until he gets into Sunday School. The church'll show him right from wrong."

Only too often both the school and the church fail because the child has not learned basic truths in the home. He has not learned unselfishness, consideration for others, or plain, ordinary kindness. These things are foundation stones of character.

Where home and school and church have failed, the police take over. The parents wail, "How could a child of ours do such a thing? We gave him everything. Yet he stole, he attacked a playmate, he tortured an old man." Yes, they gave him everything—everything but discipline. He had never been taught that other people have inalienable rights and that he must respect those rights. He did just what **he** wanted, and he grew vicious when he was refused something he wanted.

J. Edgar Hoover laments the fact that more crimes are being committed by juveniles than were committed before World War II. The type of crimes is more vicious. **Atrocities** is the only word for them, beatings, burnings, drownings.

The darkest blot on the nation's escutcheon today is juvenile crime. These crimes are of the type formerly committed by adult gangsters. Gangs exist today as in the thirties, but they are made up of youngsters, both boys and girls.

In a recent article Mr. Hoover cites several cases, the first a crime in which two teen-age youths were jailed in a gang fight in which a Navy Veteran was shot and killed, another in which a refugee was beaten and robbed, and a third in which two high school girls were stabbed. Then he quotes this incident, believable only because J. Edgar Hoover tells straight-forward, unadulterated facts.

He says, "But the most macabre—the one most indicative of the depths of the sickness permeating our social structure—is that reflecting the alleged scheduled knife-and-lead-pipe battle between two rival gangs. The sickening aspect of this incident—halted by police intervention—was the fact that the gang members were girls!"

Will this kind of girl become the mother of tomorrow? What kind of ideals can she instill into her children? Love of poetry and good books, kind neighboring, and civic cooperation?

Mr. Hoover is constantly asked for his suggestions for an effective solution, not only to solve the problem of juvenile delinquency but to solve the problem of delinquency that leads on to crime. A juvenile committing a crime is no longer in the juvenile class but in the adult category. For crime is not the exciting, glamorous thing pictured in magazines and plays. It is a sordid thing, as has been said, and Mr. Hoover can prove that not one of the criminals captured by his F.B.I. had anything to show for his life of crime. Most criminals, as has also been said before, were glad when it was all over.

What causes juvenile crime? **Authority** has become a much disliked word. A jurist recently expressed his opinion that the American father should head his household and should assume the job of disciplining his children. Mr. Hoover quotes **discipline** from Webster himself as "training which corrects, molds, strengthens and perfects." What a fine definition! It has in it no idea of punishment for its own sake but for the sake of making good rules of conduct helpful to all people, young and old.

He goes on to say that "Human beings need rules to live by—children as well as adults. ... A world without moral and legal discipline becomes a jungle of anarchy, whether it is an adult or a juvenile world."

Physical punishment has gone out of style, but it is effective when it is needed. Discipline means restriction, but parental restrictions are for the protection of the child. Mr. Hoover says of his splendid F.B.I. "We have found that discipline of the proper kind breeds efficiency, and efficiency breeds pride in achievement. This compensates for disciplinary restrictions."

Of family life he says, "Youngsters who have love, understanding, and adequate discipline in a poverty-ridden home are far less 'underprivileged' than those who may be surrounded by material wealth but who lack affection, understanding and discipline."

Everybody must recognize the difference between right and wrong. J. Edgar Hoover states it clearly. He says, "When I refer to 'right' I speak of that which is based on the moral law set forth in the Bible. Parents are eager to give freely of material gifts to their children. They should be even more generous in giving as well those things which are of inestimable value—standards, principles, and discipline."

American juveniles should, in return, accept the discipline of parents, teachers, and clergymen in a spirit of willing, even enthusiastic cooperation that we may have a better country. The law-abiding youth has a kind friend and advisor in the Director of the F.B.I. No knight in shining armor ever fought barbarism more valiantly than the modern Knight Errant, J. Edgar Hoover.

Comfort, Mildred Houghton, 1886-
    J. Edgar Hoover, modern knight errant; a biographical sketch of the director of the F. B. I.   Minneapolis, T. S. Denison [1958]

    130p.   22cm.

    1. Hoover, John Edgar, 1895-

HV7911.H6C6   923.573   58-14402‡

Library of Congress

Wakarusa
Community School
Library